Chapter One

Introduction to Intercultural Communication

● **Objectives**

➢ Understand the **chronological** development of intercultural communication.
➢ Understand the nature of intercultural communication.
➢ Understand the factors leading to the development of intercultural communication.
➢ Understand the purposes of studying intercultural communication.
➢ Understand the relationship between intercultural communication and globalization.

● **导读**

跨文化交际是指不同文化背景的人们之间的交际。跨文化交际是人类文化形成和发展过程中的固有现象。跨文化交际研究是近代美国的新兴领域,它的发展与现代传播通讯技术的改进、交通技术的发展、多媒体的诞生、经济的高度全球化、移民造成的多元文化等密切相关。

跨文化交际学是一门运用相关学科如人类学、心理学、哲学、社会学、传播学、语言学等理论和方法研究不同文化背景的人们进行交际时的交际行为和交际过程的应用性学科。跨文化交际学主要涉及交际与文化、文化感知与价值观、语言与文化、非语言与文化、跨文化适应、跨文化冲突处理和跨文化交际能力培养等内容。

Text

1.1 The Chronological Development of Intercultural Communication

The history of communication among people of different cultural backgrounds is almost as long as human history itself. The mergence and conflicts between the primitive tribes, the visits of sailors to alien lands, the bargains of merchants along the "silk road" during the Tang Dynasty in China, and the immigration of thousands upon thousands of "gold-diggers" to North America, are all examples of intercultural communication, not to say the ever-heated interaction of high officials at the United Nations since the establishment of the organization and the ever-growing wave of tourists into all corners of the world. Indeed, intercultural communication as a human activity has existed for centuries.

1.1.1 Intercultural Communication in America

Although the phenomenon of intercultural communication is as old as human society, the study of intercultural communication started in America. The very roots of intercultural communication developed initially through the study of communication. During the Second World War, military leaders were confronted with some difficulties. For example, how could allied nations cooperate with their allied officers and residents of other cultures when the leaders knew little about other languages or cultures? To solve these problems, **anthropologists** were invited to study the cultures of various nations. Thus, the study of diverse cultures aroused great concerns, setting the stage for the academic exploration of culture and communication.

Intercultural communication study as an academic field began after World War II. At that time, the United States was the leading world power, but its diplomats were ineffectual. The diplomats knew little the language of the nation to which they were assigned. In 1946, the United States Congress passed the Foreign Service Act. Later the Foreign Service Institute (FSI) was established by the U. S. Department of State to provide language and

新核心大学英语

跨文化交际学基础教程

A Foundational Coursebook on Intercultural Communication

主　编 王玉环

副主编 黄　芳 梁　伟

编　委 王彦玲 胡安琪 曲肖玉 鞠志勤 范　杰
董　晶 董　宁 高　丽 周秀霞

上海交通大学出版社
SHANGHAI JIAO TONG UNIVERSITY PRESS

内 容 提 要

本教材以培养新时代大学生跨文化交际意识、增强跨文化敏感度为目的，取材范围较广，内容丰富。本教材共分为八个单元，内容涉及跨文化交际学发展概述、文化与文化模式、价值观、环境与文化、交际与文化、语言与文化、非语言交际、跨文化适应等。本教材以阅读为主线，在理解跨文化相关理论的基础上，重点突出案例分析和练习，并补充相关的文化和知识材料、自测题等。

图书在版编目(CIP)数据

跨文化交际学基础教程/王玉环主编. —上海：上海交通大学出版社，2013(2025 重印)
(新核心大学英语)
ISBN 978-7-313-09437-7

Ⅰ.①跨… Ⅱ.①王… Ⅲ.①英语—高等学校—教材 ②文化交流—高等学校—教材 Ⅳ.①H31②G115

中国版本图书馆 CIP 数据核字(2013)第 016632 号

跨文化交际学基础教程

王玉环　主编

上海交通大学 出版社出版发行
(上海市番禺路 951 号　邮政编码 200030)
电话：64071208
浙江天地海印刷有限公司印刷　全国新华书店经销
开本：787mm×960mm　1/16　印张：14.25　字数：250 千字
2013 年 1 月第 1 版　2025 年 1 月第 7 次印刷
ISBN 978-7-313-09437-7　定价：48.00 元

前　言

20世纪以来，信息技术和交通技术的高速发展使得各种文化间的交流日益频繁。生活在当今世界“地球村”的人们，对于由文化和价值观差异产生的交际失误、矛盾和冲突有着日渐深刻的切身体会。而全球化不等于一体化，正是这些交际冲突使得人们虽近在咫尺，却又如隔天涯。

跨文化交际学是一门在传播学等学科理论的基础上，与人类学、心理学、语言学、社会学等相互交叉而发展起来的新兴学科。与欧美等国家相比，国内的跨文化交际研究与教学虽然起步较晚，但发展迅速，开设这一课程的学校日益增多，跨文化交际教学与研究已经形成了“燎原之势”。跨文化交际课程符合《国家中长期教育改革与发展规划纲要》的要求，致力于培养更多具有国际视野、了解世界文化、具备创新能力的高素质人才，符合我国外语课程标准的要求。

本教材以培养新时代大学生跨文化交际意识、增强跨文化敏感度为目的，取材范围较广，内容丰富。本教材共分为八个单元，内容涉及跨文化交际学发展概述、文化与文化模式、价值观、环境与文化、交际与文化、语言与文化、非语言交际、跨文化适应等。本教材中各单元形式基本统一，以阅读为主线，在理解跨文化相关理论的基础上，重点突出案例分析和练习,并补充相关的文化和知识材料、自测题等。

本教材编写理念新颖、内容涵盖面广,除了帮助学习者提高英语水平,还培养学习者的人文素养和跨文化能力。本教材整个编撰历经四年,其间作为英语专业本科限选课和大学英语公共选修课教材使用了三年,现教材是在师生的意见反馈和同行的宝贵意见基础上反复修改而定稿的。建议将该教材用于大学英语必修课的教学课时为50～60学时,选修课可根据教学实际需要,选取最为重要的章节讲授,相应缩短学时,以满足不同层次学生的教学要求。

本人曾两次赴加拿大访学,从事跨文化交际教学与研究。本书编者都是从事跨文化交际教学的一线教师及研究者,具有丰富的课堂教学以及教材编写的经验,她们为本教材的编写付出了辛苦的劳动。衷心地感谢所有参与本教材编写的老师们!

鉴于我们的水平和能力有限,书中的疏漏之处仍在所难免,恳请各位专家、学者以及本教材的使用者批评指正,以便我们今后进一步改进和完善。

王玉环

2012年10月

Contents

anthropological cultural training for foreign diplomats. Following the Second World War, programs focusing on world situations and international policy have influenced the development of intercultural communication studies. With the establishment of the United Nations in 1945, governments initiated new organizations such as the World Health Organization, the United Nation's assistance programs, the World Bank, and other agencies, which generated a need to understand the cultures of various countries.

The United States Congress passed a Act 1953 instituting the United States Information Agency (USIA). The name was changed in 1977 to the International Communication Agency (ICA). This agency was charged with providing information about the United States through various communication media to nations of the world. The broadcast "Voice of America" exemplified those efforts.

During 1950s, early pioneers such as Edward T. Hall, the father of the field of intercultural communication study, found that the USIA lacked cultural information. While associated with the Foreign Service Institute, Hall applied abstract anthropological concepts to the practical world to include communication.

Hall **conceptualize**d the new field of intercultural communication (ICC) in the early 1950s when he worked for the U.S. Foreign Service Institute. During this decade, Edward Y. Hall drew upon his vast experience with the Hopi and Navaho Indians during the 1930s and 1940s and with the help of foreign service officers in the USIA, he wrote the classic *The Silent Language*. The term "intercultural communication" itself did not appear until Hall's *The Silent language* was published in 1959, in which he popularized the new area of communication. This book paved the way for the study of intercultural communication by showing how culture is critical to understanding intercultural communication. Hall went on with the studies on intercultural communication and published the following books such as *The Hidden Dimension* (1966), *Beyond Culture* (1976), *The Dance of Life* (1984), and *Understanding Cultural Differences* (1989), all of which have influenced the development of the field of intercultural communication.

The 1960s was the period of conceptualization of ICC by communication scholars. The 1960s also marked a cultural awakening decade. With the institution of Civil Rights Act in 1964, America discovered the roots of multiculturalism. The same decade gave birth to many human rights issues in the United States. The social problems and the conflicts made Americans aware that communication between groups and cultures was an urgent domestic issue.

The 1970s saw rapid development in the field, reflected in the publication of numerous studies. Intercultural communication was offered as a course of study in many American universities since then.

During the 1980s the field moved toward integration and a clearer identity. The 1990s, stressing diversification of methods and displaying increasing concern with domestic co-cultures in the United States, had also witnessed efforts to redress historical and colonial imbalance.

From the 1970s to the present time, the direction for the study of intercultural communication has been determined mainly by three influences: ⓐ the international and intercultural Communication Annual (IICA), ⓑ the Speech Communication Association (SCA), and ⓒ the International Communication Association (ICA). SCA and ICA are the two major professional associations for communication study in the USA.

In the past 50 years, the field of intercultural communication has developed both theoretically and practically. Theoretically, the study of intercultural communication focuses on purposeful interaction between people of different cultures and different racial and **ethnic** groups. Practically, intercultural communication is applied in different kinds of intercultural and interethnical training programs to help people from different backgrounds understand and accept each other in academic, business, government, and other settings.

1.1.2 Intercultural Communication in China

The history of intercultural communication study in China is much shorter and more recent than that in the United States and Europe. The awareness and study of intercultural communication started in 1980s when some foreign English teachers took an interest in intercultural communication for the purpose of changing traditional teaching methodology to communicative approach in EFL in China. Later, some English teachers became interested in the field when they began to explore the relationships between language and culture. The process can be divided into four periods:

(1) The years of 1979 to 1987 marked the first period, when there was a heavy emphasis on foreign language teaching.

(2) The years of 1988 to 1994 marked the second period, while foreign language teaching was still growing and being emphasized. Intercultural Communication as a new discipline began to draw attention among Chinese researchers. Intercultural communication was taught as a course for English major students in many universities.

(3) The third period began in 1995 when the 5th International Conference on Cross-cultural Communication "East and West" was held in China; and it was during this conference that the China Association for the Intercultural Communication was established.

(4) The fourth period has lasted from 2000 to the present. In the past decade, many books on intercultural communication written by scholars abroad were introduced into China. Some books written by Chinese scholars in this field were published as well. Intercultural communication as an academic field has been recognized by scholars, and some international and national conferences are held each year, which pushed the development of this field in China.

In short, intercultural communication began as a serious discipline for study with China's reform and opening up initiatives. Since China's entry into WTO, trade and communication across the borders are increasingly recognized as a daily routine. China's winning the bid to host the 2008 Olympics and 2010 World Expo is another great success that greatly enhances intercultural interactions between China and the world. Chinese scholars have focused on their researches in intercultural communication academically and practically with the fast pace of development in China.

1.2 The Nature of Intercultural Communication

Intercultural communication is the "interaction between people whose cultural perceptions and symbol systems are distinct enough to alter the communication event" (Samovar and Porter, 2004). "Intercultural communication is a symbolic, interpretive, transactional, contextual process in which the degree of difference between people is large and important enough to create dissimilar interpretations and expectations about what are regarded as competent behaviors that should be used to create shared meanings" (Lustig & Koester 1996).

Intercultural communication is based on theoretical research achievement of many relative branches. It includes interethnic communication, interracial communication, intracultural communication and international intercultural communication, etc. It touches on various fields. They are mainly concerned about the cultural orientation, conception of values, social norms, way of thinking, various differences in encoding and decoding process, verbal and nonverbal behaviors, and the usage of international language and discourse organization.

Intercultural communication is a cross branch which develops on the basis of common communication, while based on scientific theory and facts, the branch also displays the dynamic process and explores its nature, rules and factors that influence social cultures, minds, situations, contexts etc. This branch shows the cultural differences in communicative process in different cultural context so as to raise people's sensibility to cultural difference.

Intercultural communication is an exciting field of study in many ways. It explores cultural and group influence on communication. The study of intercultural communication recognizes how culture pervades what we are, how we act, how we think, and how we talk and listen. It indicates how we are socialized into a cultural context, and how culture influences our interaction along with many other areas such as work, gender expectations, and health.

It is certain that there exist some problems and differences in the international trading, education, resources, management, public affairs, business, environmental protection, universal exploration, science and technology among nations. All of these issues cause some cultural conflicts, misunderstandings and even disasters. It is these issues and conflicts that make the study of intercultural communication more important.

1.3 Factors Leading to the Development of Intercultural Communication

There are many factors contributing to the development of intercultural communication. Among them, three trends combine to **usher** in a more interdependent future that shape our differences into a set of shared concerns and a common agenda: technological development, globalization of the economy, and widespread population migration.

1.3.1 Technological Development

Technological changes have made the world a smaller planet to inhabit. The technological feasibility of the mass media that brings events from across the globe into our home, school, office dramatically shortens the distance between peoples of different cultures and societies.

The improvement of information technology such as internet, the cellphone, cable TV systems, has greatly reshaped intercultural communication, creating common meanings and a reliance on persons we may or may not meet face-to-face at some future date in our lives. Telecommunication systems link the world via satellites and fiber optics. Many world events are experienced almost instantaneously and are no longer separated from us in time and space. People could watch the wonderful 2012 Olympic games held in London in front of TV or computer at home. Scenes of an earthquake in China, a typhoon in Philippines or a **tsunamis** in Japan were viewed on TV or internet all over the world.

In the past fifteen years, the number of cellphone users has grown from virtually zero to more than two billion people. Internet users have exceeded 1.5 billion people. The internet has radically transformed the ways people interact with each other. Family members who are widely **dispersed** across the globe are able to maintain contact, thus helping to sustain the culture's beliefs, value, norms, and social practices. A counterpoint to this consequence of the internet is its availability for introducing new ideas and images into cultures, which may speed up and change the nature of the culture itself.

Modern transportation systems contribute to the creation of the global village. **Supersonic** aircrafts carry people from one country to another faster than the speed of sound. A visit to major cities such as New York, Shanghai, Mexico City, London, Tokyo, Hong Kong, Paris, has become commonplace.

We ride the wave of information that **surges** about the globe. We sit in our living room but keep connections to events that happen elsewhere in the world. The immediacy of our new technology builds in us a new sense of national and global commonality.

1.3.2 Economic Development

The progress of communication and transportation technology has made markets more accessible and the world of business more globally interdependent in past decades. The trend toward a global economy brings people and products together from around the world.

The ability to interact with people from different cultures has immense economic benefits. For instance, the economic success of the United States in the world increasingly depends on individual and collective abilities to communicate competently with people from other cultures. U. S. international trade has more than doubled every decade since 1960. U. S. trade as a percentage of gross world products rises from 15 percent in 1986 to nearly 27 percent in 2006. In 2007, U. S. trade with China, the United States' second leading trade partner, accounts for nearly $500 billion in trade. In 2010, the U. S. trade with the top 10 countries with which the United States trade accounts for nearly $3 trillion. Take China as another example, China has expanded international trading since 1978. In 2011, China's import and export total amount is about $2.97 trillion. Only through successful intercultural communication can such economic potentials be realized.

In the face of economic globalization, nations must determine how to remain competitive in the presence of new trade communities and must find ways to promote products and services. Companies in many industries today operate in a global marketplace. They design products to fit a wide diversity of cultures, advertise them in numerous languages, and meet the demands of very different consumers.

Globalization of the economy leads to a more uniform way of conducting business. The interdependence among national economies **hinges** on effective intercultural communication and calls for ever more skillful interaction in the future across national boundaries. Greater cultural and ethnic understanding becomes necessary both to carry out world business and to preserve cultural diversity.

1.3.3 Widespread Population Migration

The world is currently in the midst of what is perhaps the largest and most extensive wave of cultural mixing in recorded history. There is no doubt that the United States of America stood out in terms of cultural mixing. In recent decades, successive waves of immigration have rewoven the fabric of American society. Much of the U. S. population can be attributed to immigration. In 2003, about 33.5 million people — or about 11% of the U.S. population — were immigrants. In 2008, there are approximately 303 million people in the United States (roughly 4.5% of the world's total population). Of these people, nearly 66.8% are European American, 14.8% are **Latino**, 12.8% are African American, 4.6% are Asian American, and 1% is Native American. America was considered to be a "melting pot" of ethnicities; more recently, this image has been replaced by that of the "tossed salad" or "**mosaic**".

Because of immigration trends, cultural and ethnic diversity in the United States is a fact of life. Recent data clearly show that the United States is now a multicultural society. About 18% of the people in the United States speak a language other than English at home. Of children in urban public schools, one-third of them speak a first language other than English. In the public schools of New York City, more than 160 different languages are spoken. In the city of Los Angles, more than 100 different languages are spoken.

The United States is not alone in the worldwide transformation into multicultural societies. Throughout Europe, Asia, Africa, South America, and the Middle East, there is an increasing pattern of cross-border movements that is both changing the distribution of people around the globe and **intensify**ing the political and social tensions that accompany such population shifts.

1.4 Purposes of Studying Intercultural Communication

The accelerating globalization process and the growing contact of people from different cultures in the shrinking world of the 21st century have forced people to pay even more attention to intercultural issues such as misunderstandings, low intolerance of different cultural conventions, and language barriers.

People are the key complex component in all communication within and across cultures because they communicate their cultures along with the message. It is the human factor that affects intercultural communication.

Acquiring the knowledge and skills of intercultural communication is a priority to people in becoming a global citizen of the 21st century. The reality of the global village challenges all its residents to develop a broader worldview, a more global psychology, and the cultural skills necessary for building relationships and solving problems. Therefore, the benefits of studying intercultural communication are as follows:

- It may develop the understanding of cultures to appreciate the opportunities and challenges that each culture presents and learn how individuals have dealt with those opportunities and challenges.
- It may expand the range of verbal and nonverbal communication skills and enhance the ability to select and perform communication behaviors appropriate to various settings.
- It may enhance the understanding of cultural variability and positive emotion to search for a common ground of multicultural coexistence.
- It may help people promote their holistic self-development and learn to observe, experience, reflect, evaluate, summarize and communicate evidence with fairness, clarity, accuracy, precision, and thoroughness.
- It may enlarge the intercultural vision with sensitivity, understanding,

tolerance, accommodation, **empathy** and respect.

With rapid changes in global economy, technology, transportation, and immigration policies, the world is becoming a small, intersecting community. We find ourselves in increasing contact with people who are culturally different, working side by side with us. From workplace to classroom, different cultural beliefs, values, and communication styles are here to stay. In order to achieve effective intercultural communication, we have to learn to manage differences flexibly and mindfully. In sum, in a world of international interdependence, the ability to understand and communicate effectively with people from other cultures is of great necessity.

1.5 Globalization and Intercultural Communication

Marshall Mcluhan (1962) characterizes today's world as a "global village" to describe how scientific and technological advances of mass media would eventually disintegrate the natural time and space barriers inherent in human communication. At the dawn of the 21st century, the vision of a global village is no longer considered an abstract idea but a near certainty. Technological and sociopolitical changes have made the world a smaller planet to inhabit.

Globalization has shrunk the world. This is especially true due to the impact of new communication technologies such as the Internet. The world today is therefore globally integrated, interrelated and interdependent. A global cultural flow in social, technical, cultural, political and ecological spheres has changed the international landscape and the way people communicate. It has had an enormous impact upon the intercultural understanding and behavior.

These dimensions — migration, media, technology, finance and ideology — have combined to establish a new world in which people share concerns over global issues and expect to make joint efforts to address issues such as poverty, health, environment, climate change, terrorism, sea-piracy, drugs, ect. Tackling these issues requires a global mindset and cooperation in decision-making and problem-solving. Most important of all, the issues require people to become aware of all the areas of intercultural communication if they choose to be global citizens. New information and communication technology, as well as fast and effective transport systems, connect people around the world. In this way, people become exposed to various opportunities to integrate both local and global perspectives in intercultural communication and to share their concerns as a global community.

Intercultural communication involves interaction with people from different cultural backgrounds. The cultural flow in the form of migration, media, finance, technology and ideology has quickened the pace of globalization. As migrant populations seek employment, education, investment opportunities and new spaces to enjoy better security and a peaceful coexistence, the socio-political goal of building global communities will remain a very significant phase of their lives. The process of globalization is therefore forcing people as global citizens to rethink their intercultural communication strategies to bridge cultural differences and address their common concerns by building a global community.

New Words and Phrases

chronological /ˈkrɒnəˈlɒdʒɪkəl/ *adj*. 按时间顺序的
anthropologist /ˌænθrəˈpɒlədʒɪst/ *n*. 人类学家
conceptualize /kənˈseptjʊəlaɪz/ *vt*. 概念化
ethnic /ˈeθnɪk/ *adj*. 人种的,种族的
usher /ˈʌʃə/ *vt*. 引导,护送 *n*. 带位员,招待员
tsunami /tsʊˈnɑːmi/ *n*. 海啸
disperse /dɪsˈpɜːs/ *vt*. 传播,散开 *vi*. 分散
supersonic /ˈsjuːpəˈsɒnɪk/ *adj*. 超声波的 *n*. 超声波
surge /sɜːdʒ/ *n*. 汹涌,澎湃 *v*. 汹涌,涌起,暴涨
hinge /hɪndʒ/ *n*. 铰链,关键 *vt*. 用铰链装 *vi*. 依情况而定 (on)
latino /ləˈtiːnəʊ/ *adj*. 拉丁美洲的;拉丁美洲人的 *n*. 拉丁美洲人
mosaic /məˈzeɪɪk/ *n*. 马赛克

intensify /ɪn'tensɪfai/ *vt*. 使加强，使强化；使变激烈
empathy /'empəθi/ *n*. 神入；移情作用

Exercises

I. Questions for discussion

1. What does globalization mean?
2. What are the trends that make our world more interdependent?
3. What is the relationship between the technological superhighway and intercultural communication?
4. Which current technologies do you think affect and change your culture most? How so?
5. How do you think the ever-present cellphone, as a medium to communicate with others, will change interpersonal relationships?

II. Multiple choice

Directions: *Choose the best answer to each of the following questions*.

1. Intercultural communication is the exchange of information between individuals who are unalike ________.

   A. culturally　　B. physically
   C. psychologically　　D. mentally

2. Among the following choices, which is **not** the major factor that contributes to the development of intercultural communication? ________

   A. technological development　　B. globalization of the economy
   C. population migration　　D. improved living standard

3. Which is **not** the major purpose of learning ICC? ________

   A. Develop understanding of culture to appreciate opportunities and challenges.
   B. Learn as many languages as possible.
   C. Expand communication skills and ability to be appropriate to various settings.
   D. Forge an intercultural vision to deal with culture shock.

4. Intercultural communication as a discipline first started in ________.

   A. Japan.　　B. France　　C. China　　D. America

5. Intercultural communication refers to the decoding and encoding of information that comes from people from ______ cultural background.

A. the same B. local C. different D. national

III. Fill in the blanks with the words given below

__(1)__ communication is a form of __(2)__ communication. It is used to describe the wide range of communication problems that naturally appear within an organization made up of individuals from different religious, social, ethnic, and educational __(3)__. In this sense it seeks to understand how people from different countries and cultures act, communicate and perceive the world around them.

Many people in intercultural business communication argue that culture __(4)__ how individuals __(5)__ messages, what mediums they choose for __(6)__ them, and the way messages are __(7)__. As a separate notion, it studies situations where people from different cultural backgrounds __(8)__. Aside from language, intercultural communication focuses on social attributes, thought __(9)__, and the cultures of different groups of people. It also involves understanding the different cultures, languages and customs of people from other countries. Intercultural communication plays a __(10)__ in social sciences such as anthropology, cultural studies, linguistics, psychology and communication studies. Intercultural communication is also referred to as the base for international businesses.

(1) A. cultural B. intercultural C. cross-cultural D. racial

(2) A. national B. community C. local D. global

(3) A. locations B. beliefs C. backgrounds D. degrees

(4) A. determines B. follows C. learns D. discovers

(5) A. decode B. encode C. see D. send

(6) A. interpreting B. receiving
C. transmitting D. understanding

(7) A. interpreted B. referred C. accepted D. understood

(8) A. see B. interact C. talk D. think

(9) A. behaviors B. understandings
C. methods D. patterns

(10) A. role B. game C. foundation D. joke

Case Study

Case I

Wang Lin is a new teacher in a middle school. One day, Li Qing, her Chinese colleague, introduces her to a middle-aged teacher from America. Helen is teaching English in this school.

Liu: Wang Lin, this is Helen, our English teacher from America. And Helen, this is Wang Lin, a new mathematics teacher.

Wang: How do you do?

Helen: Hi. Your skirt is beautiful.

Wang: No, it is old. I bought it two years ago.

Helen: You look pretty and smart. I am sure you are a good teacher.

Wang: No, no. I'm just a new teacher. I should learn from you old teacher.

Helen: Do you think I'm old? (With a surprised look)

Questions for Discussion

1. What are the different cultural orientations of social relations revealed in the dialogue?
2. What value do the negative responses to compliments show?
3. How do you usually respond to others' compliments on your appearance?

Case Analysis

This case reflects different cultural orientations and communicative behaviors between Chinese and Americans. Both parties communicate from their own cultural perspectives and thus cause some misunderstanding.

Wang Lin comes from a collectivistic culture. Chinese social relations orientation stresses respects to the old and formality. She displays her humbleness by saying she should learn from Helen, an old teacher, and shows her respect to Helen with a formal greeting and modesty after Helen says she is beautiful and smart. While Helen comes from an individualistic culture. American social relations orientation emphasizes equality, informality and directness. That's why Helen replies to Wang's greeting with an informal way and makes compliments on Wang's appearance at their first meeting.

Individualistic cultures do not associate as much deference with age as collectivistic cultures do. Therefore, Helen is surprised when told she is an old teacher. She does not know that the word "old" has an connotation "experienced" in Chinese. In America, being old means being useless.

The case also reflects that culture influences communication. When Helen compliments Wang on her beautiful skirt and pretty look and intelligence, she is very direct and honest. It is a typical American communicative style. Wang responds to the compliments by giving negative responses "No, no." And she displays her humbleness by saying that her skirt was bought two years ago. The negative responses to honest compliments would certainly puzzle Helen.

Case II

Mr. Carpenter, an American salesman in ABP company, has been having business negotiations with Mr. Sato, a Japanese businessman for three days. Many details about the business have been discussed. Now there is only one problem left — the delivery date.

Mr. Carpenter: I'd like to come back to the question of the delivery date again. We seem to have skipped over that one.

Mr. Sato: Yes. This is a slightly complicated issue. It will take some thought.

Mr. Carpenter: Not really. It's just a matter of choosing a date. All of us here can agree on.

Mr. Sato: Yes, choosing a date.

Mr. Carpenter: I think three months after the start of production is reasonable. What do you think?

Mr. Sato: Yes. Three months. Very reasonable. Perhaps we can take a break now.

Mr. Carpenter: A break? Right now? We only have this one item left and then we'll be finished, if we could just decide.

Mr. Sato: Yes, we need to decide, if we could just have a break.

Mr. Carpenter: OK. But let's make it quick.

Questions for Discussion

1. Why do Japanese usually use indirect communicative style?
2. Why do Americans usually use direct communicative style?
3. What kind of communicative styles do you often use in your daily communication?

Case Analysis

This case illustrates the different communicative styles between Japanese and Americans. In Japan, interpersonal communication is based on a great deal of guessing and reading between the lines. Directness is disagreeable. A speaker's intentions are hidden or hinted during interaction. In America, People using a direct communicative style generally employ overt expressions of intention. Americans tend to verbalize the messages to make their intentions clear and explicit. Americans are encouraged to "speak their mind."

In the dialogue, Mr. Carpenter makes his suggestion to settle the delivery time immediately. For some reasons, Mr. Sato is reluctant to make a quick agreement on the delivery date. He frequently uses breaks to work out compromises to avoid public displays of disagreement. The first and most obvious example is when Mr. Sato says that this is "a slightly complicated issue" that will "take some thought." In fact, this is a signal that the subject is not appropriate for open discussion at this time. However, Mr. Carpenter does not understand that.

Further Reading

Reading I

Globalization in its Universal Dimensions

Globalization may be defined as the increasing scale, extent, variety, speed, and magnitude of international cross-border, social, economic, military, political, and cultural interrelations. Globalization means we are all parts of a steadily shrinking and interdependent world. Business dealings that were once confined primarily to local economies have given way to an extensive integrated world economy. Information that once traveled through time-consuming methods now appears in the blink of an eye across a wide range of media. People are becoming more mobile than ever and more likely to traverse into cultures different from their own. Literally and figuratively, the walls that separate us are tumbling down. Though we may not have fully become a "global village," there is no denying that the various cultures of the world are far more accessible than ever before, and that the peoples of these cultures are coming into contact at an ever-increasing rate.

Globalization has always been with us. Ever since the first humans left their places of origin and began multiplying, spreading, and eventually migrating to other continents, globalization has been a fact of life. Historically, globalization has been promoted by war and conquest, by religious conversion, by migration and colonization, by the new introduction of new tools and agricultural techniques, by literacy and invention of the printing press, by disease and its prevention. It is obvious that globalization can be a force for good (literacy, economic development, higher living standards) as well as for destruction (war, famine, AIDS).

Globalization is a product of the industrial revolution. Britain grew rich in the 19th century as the first global economic superpower, because of its superior manufacturing technology and improved global communications such as steamships and railroads. In recent decades, the pace, spread, and impact of globalization have accelerated beyond anything experienced in past history. The rapid spread of information technology and the internet is changing the way companies organize production, and increasingly allowing services as well as manufacturing to be globalized. Modern transportation and communications have brought about great changes. For example, travel that takes months in the past takes hours now. It takes hundreds of years for the effects of Columbus's discovery of America to be fully felt, however, it has taken only thirty-two years for China's great economic boom to have a global impact on trade and financial market. Hence, globalization and its impact are faster, broader, and deeper than ever before.

Globalization takes many different forms: economic, political, military, cultural, as well as technological form. In economic terms, globalization refers to the growing economic integration of the world when trade, investment and money increasingly cross international borders. Trade has been the engine of globalization, with world trade in manufactured goods increasing more than 100 times (from $95 billion to $12 trillion) in the past 50 years since 1955, much faster than the overall growth of the world economy. For example, at least one-third of the U. S. economy is now generated by international trade. The total amount of import and export in China in 2012 is $3 866.7 billion. Politically, when the United States seeks to export its concepts abroad, that too is globalization. Culturally, when people export their movies, television programs, language, blue jeans, rock music, and so on, they are acting as agents of globalization. And, of course, technologically, computers, the World-wide Web, iPods, cellphones, faxes and telephones are key instruments of globalization.

The world has become a smaller place. More and more countries and people are being integrated into a globalized market economy. Whether your purchases are automobiles from Japan, fresh flowers from Columbia, shoes from Italy, fresh grapes from Chile, or any of the thousands of other products, this is all part of globalization. If you say you wish to buy an "American car," the chances are the transmission is made in Mexico, the frame produced in Japan, the parts manufactured in Central America, and only assembly done in the United States. Is that really an American car or is it something else: another product of globalization?

Nowadays, more and more of what we used to think of as our "national economy" has become international. By and large, this is a good thing — we get better products and better service at a lower price. Lots of people benefit: developed countries like the United States can maintain a high standard of living, while in developing countries many new jobs are created, new technologies are introduced, salaries increase, money starts to flow, and prosperity increases. Moreover, there is a multiplier effect: economists estimate that for every dollar that a country invests in international trade, it receives two dollars in return.

Globalization may carry potential drawbacks. We are just as likely to

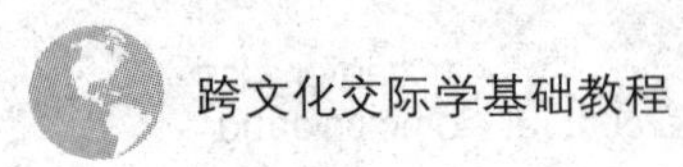

become a global battlefield as we are to become a global village or a global community. The twentieth century was the bloodiest in human history, with ethnic cleansing, two world wars, and hundreds of inter and intra-national wars. The terrorist attacks of September 11, 2001, on the World Trade Center in New York and the Pentagon in Washington, D.C., and the Iraqi War have changed the context of global social relations. At present, we are living in a state of constant terror.

Although globalization is a unifying influence with worldwide force, it impacts countries in various ways. The effects of globalization don't move in one direction. Increasingly, the process is a two-way street: we affect others through globalization and we, in turn, are affected by it. Globalization makes us both dependent on the rest of the world for oil, manufactured goods, and raw materials, but it also makes us and other countries interdependent in all kinds of complex ways.

In general, globalization improves our lives. Few of us would really want to give up jet travel, cellphones, widescreen televisions, computers, and the opportunities for new experiences that are so much a part of our lives and that are also the products of globalization. But not everyone is a winner; globalization creates losers as well. What to do about those people — small farmers, shop owners, those thrown out of work by job replacement — can only be resolved democratically and in the political process.

In the words of Robert Muller (1997), former UN Under-Secretary General, we ought:

> To see the world with global eyes;
> To love the world with a global heart;
> To understand the world with a global spirit.

Reading II

Metaphors of U.S. Cultural Diversity

Many cultural groups live within the borders of the United Sates. When people talk about the blend of U. S. cultural groups, their ideas are often condensed into a few key words or phrases. These summary images, called metaphors, imply both descriptions of what is and, less obviously, prescriptions of what should be. The following three metaphors are often used to describe the cultural mix within the United States: a melting pot, a set of **tributaries** (支流的), and a garden salad.

The Melting Pot Metaphor

In 1914 a Broadway theater play, *The Melting Pot*, presented the notion that the United States was becoming a superior society because of its **fusion** (融合) of cultures. Many people believed that immigrants who came to the United States would, within a relatively short period of time, cast aside their original identities, cultures, and languages as they were forced to adopt the loyalties, customs, and languages of their new home. It was assumed that immigrants would all be **assimilate**d (被同化) rapidly — absorbed and blended with mainstream U. S. society. Henry Ford hired thousands of new immigrants to build his Model Ts. He required all of them to participate in a ceremony on stage where they would climb a ladder into a giant pot in the costumes of their original cultures. As they emerged from the other side of the pot, they would be dressed as "Americans."

Since then, the melting pot metaphor has been used to describe multiple cultures in the United States. According to this image, America is like a huge container that can withstand extremely high temperatures and can therefore be used to melt, mix, and ultimately fuse together metals or other substances. This image is the dominant way to represent the ideal blending of cultural groups at a time when the hardened steel that was forged in the great blast furnaces of Pittsburgh helped to make the United States into an industrial power. According to this view, immigrants from many cultures came to the United States to work, live, mix, and blend together into one great assimilated culture.

Dynamic as the melting pot metaphor has been in the United States, but it has never been an accurate description. The tendency for diverse cultures to melt together and assimilate their unique heritage into a single cultural entity has never really existed. Rather, the many cultural groups within the

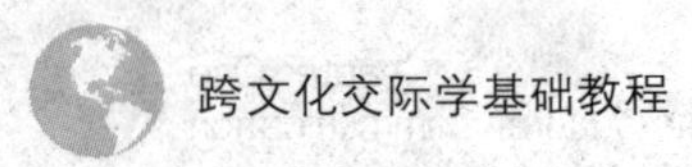

United States have continuously adapted to one another as they accommodate and perhaps adopt some of the practices and preferences of other groups while maintaining their own unique and distinctive heritages.

Today, the United States is a nation composed of an incredibly diverse set of immigration cultures that do not seem to be "melting." As noted in the following part, a more accurate metaphor is "tributary streams" or a "garden salad," as immigrants maintain their native cultures while adapting to life in another society.

The Tributaries Metaphor

A currently popular metaphor for describing the mix of cultures in the United States are tributary streams. America, according to this image, is like a huge cultural watershed, providing numerous paths in which many tributary cultures can flow. The tributaries maintain their unique identities as they surge toward their common destination. This view is useful and compelling. Unlike the melting pot metaphor, which implies that all cultures in the United States ought to be blended to overcome their individual weakness, the tributary image seems to suggest that it is acceptable and desirable for cultural groups to maintain their unique identities.

However, when the metaphor of tributaries is examined closely, there are objections to some of its implications. Further, the idea of tributaries blending together to form one main stream suggests that the tributaries are somehow subordinate to or less important than the mighty river into which they flow.

Tributary streams are small, secondary creeks that ultimately flow into a common stream, where they combine to form a major river. The difficulty with this notion rests in the hidden assumption that the cultural groups will ultimately and inevitably blend together into a single, common current. Indeed, there are far fewer examples of cultures that have totally been assimilated into the mainstream U. S. culture than there are instances of cultures that have remained unique.

The Garden Salad Metaphor

Like a garden salad made up of many distinct ingredients that are being tossed continuously, some people see the United States as made up of a complex array of distinct cultures that are blended into a unique and tasteful mixture. The substitution of one **ingredient**（原料，要素）for another，or even the change of each ingredient，and the entire flavor of the salad may be changed. Mix the salad differently and the look and feel will also differ. A salad contains a blend of ingredients，and it provides a unique combination of tints，textures，and tastes that tempt the palate.

Like the other metaphors，the garden salad is not without its flaws. A garden salad suggests an absence of firmness and stability. It has no fixed arrangement；it is always in a state of **flux**（流动，变迁）. Cultural groups in the United States，however，are not always moving，mixing，and mingling with the speed and **alacrity**（敏捷，轻快）that the metaphor would suggest. Nevertheless，this metaphor is recommended as the one that is likely to be most useful in characterizing the diversity of cultural groups in the United States.

Chapter Two

Culture and Cultural Patterns

● **Objectives**

➢ Understand the nature and characteristics of culture.

➢ Understand the nature and components of cultural patterns.

➢ Understand five cultural orientations.

● **导读**

文化是一种社会现象，是人们长期生产创造形成的产物。同时，文化又是一种历史现象，是社会历史的积淀物。确切地说，文化是指一个国家或民族的历史、地理、风土人情、传统习俗、生活方式、文学艺术、行为规范、思维方式、价值观念等。

文化模式分为特殊的文化模式和普遍的文化模式两类。特殊的文化模式是指各民族或国家具有的独特的文化体系。如以农业为主的经济，众多的农村人口、浓厚的家族观念、重人伦、对祖宗及传统权威的崇拜等互相联系形成了中国传统的文化模式；工商业发达的资本主义经济，以城市生活为主导，个人主义、总统制等互相联系而形成了美国的文化模式。普遍的文化模式包括九个部分：语言、物质特质、美术、神话与科学知识、宗教习惯、家庭与社会体制、财产、政府和战争。

文化具有超时空的稳定性和很强的凝聚力，一个民族的文化模式一经形成，必然会持久地支配每个社会成员的思想和行为。

Text

2.1 Culture

Culture is the total accumulation of beliefs, customs, values, behaviors, institutions and communication patterns that are shared, learned and passed down through the generations in an identified group of people.

2.1.1 Nature of Culture

The word "culture" has numerous meanings, ranging from biological growth, to personal refinement, literature and fine arts, patterns for living, and way of life. In English there are two normal uses of the word: high culture, and the anthropological concept of culture. High culture focuses on intellectual and artistic achievements. One might speak of a city as having a great deal of culture because there are many art exhibits, concert performances, and public lectures. The Tang Dynasty (AD 618—907) in Chinese history is generally regarded as a period of high culture.

The study of intercultural communication is concerned with **anthropological** culture. When the word "culture" is used in its anthropological sense, it means that culture is any of the customs, worldviews, languages, kinship systems, social organizations, and other taken-for-granted day-to-day practices of a people which set that group apart as a distinctive group. Specifically, the term "culture" in American anthropology has two meanings: ① the evolved human capacity to classify and represent experiences with symbols, and to act imaginatively and creatively; and ② the distinct ways that people living in different parts of the world classify and represent their experiences, and act creatively.

To understand a culture, people need to understand all the experiences that guide its individual members through life, such things as languages, gestures, personal appearance, social relationships, religions, philosophy, values, courtship, marriage, family customs, food, recreation, education, communication systems, health, transportation, government systems, and economic systems.

Culture is complex in nature because it is constantly changing. For instance, migrant populations need to adapt to new ideas and values in the dominant culture they move into, while they still keep most of the features of their original culture. This adaptation to new or dominant cultures is referred to as acculturation. Also, culture is integrated systems. Culture is deeply rooted in, affected by, connected to, and dependent on other parts and processes of a system.

2.1.2 Characteristics of Culture

There are six basic characteristics of culture: being holistic, learned, **dynamic**, shared, pervasive, and created.

First, culture is holistic. As a holistic system, culture can be divided into several subsystems, such as an educational system, a political system, an economic system, a kinship system, a religious system, and so on. The various aspects of culture are closely interrelated. In other words, any change in a subsystem will affect the whole system. For example, in 1978, China's reform and opening up policy, which brought about changes in economic and political systems altered the attitudes, values, and behaviors of the Chinese people.

Second, culture is learned. Since culture is a shared symbolic system within a relatively large group of people, the only way for group members to integrate into, reinforce, and co-create this shared symbolic system is a process through learning. People begin to learn their culture consciously and unconsciously since childhood from family members, school teachers and peers. Interacting with them is the most common way to learn about their culture. Other channels for learning are schools, newspaper, internet, church, art, etc.

Third, culture is dynamic. Culture is constantly changing over time. Culture changes in the process of transmission from generation to generation, group to group, and place to place. Four major mechanisms account for the change of culture: technological inventions, disasters, cultural contacts, and environmental factors. Technical inventions update our culture, such as the invention and use of communication tools and transportation vehicles like computers, internets and fast speed planes. Disasters include natural and human calamities. The American Civil War and China's Opium War led to great social and cultural changes to both countries. Cultural exchange gives each culture a chance to learn from each other. For example, Italian pizzas and Chinese egg rolls have become popular in America. American fast foods and pop music have greatly changed the way Asian people live. As for environmental factors, an example is that of the increasing population, which has expanded the size of cities and reduced the size of farmlands. The result is that an industrial lifestyle has taken the place of the traditional agricultural living patterns. The change completely alters the way people initiate, maintain, and terminate interpersonal relationships.

Fourth, culture is shared. What members of a culture share includes values and beliefs, customs, language, gestures or certain foods and ways of eating. They may also share a distinctive history and artifacts as well as an artistic tradition including music, literature and folk stories.

Fifth, culture is pervasive. Culture penetrates into every aspect of our life and influences the way we think, the way we talk, and the way we behave. Culture combines visible and invisible things around us. Culture has a direct influence on the physical, rational, and perceptual environment. For example, the physical arrangement of classrooms, the social relationship between students and teachers vary significantly from culture to culture.

Finally, culture is created. Each group or population creates its own values, norms, behaviors, and material objects that they feel best to their situations. The material objects produced by means of a culture, together with its musical and artistic productions, are referred to as cultural artifacts. American products such as Disneyland, rock and roll, McDonald's, and so forth well reflect American culture and are popular all over the world.

Culture is the software of the human mind that provides an operating environment for human behaviors. Although individual behaviors may be varied, all members within the same operating environment share important characteristics of the culture.

2.1.3 Whole Culture and Subculture

There are many groups and communities in different regions in this world. People in these groups or communities share the same or similar values or viewpoints of the world, the life mode, which form and develop their own special culture and relative communication culture. We may classify the general culture into two categories — whole culture and subculture.

Whole culture stands for the whole nation/people in one country such as Chinese culture, American culture, or Canadian culture. It is the mainstream culture of a society. It involves the cultural components common to most members of the society. It includes the views of politics, conceptions of self and others, basic roles, standard forms of speech, and general norms that most people in the society are aware of and accept.

Subculture is a culture existing in whole culture. It is shared by minority. Subcultures are variations of the dominant culture that exists in a society. Subcultures can be ethnic, regional, occupational, social economical, religious or gender-related in nature. For example, the IBM Corporation has a distinctive organizational culture in which male employees are expected to wear dark blue suits, white button-down shirts, and conservative neckties. People such as the elder, poor, illiterate, homosexual have their own special modes of behavior, norms, concept of time, values of life, mode of acquisition, which are different from the whole culture. In China, we have northern culture, southern culture, Tibetan culture, youth culture, woman culture, etc. In the United States, there is black culture, Hispanic culture, rural culture, etc.

2.2 Cultural Patterns

Shared beliefs, values, norms and social practices that are stable over time and that lead to roughly similar behaviors across similar situations are known as cultural patterns. (Lustig, 1996)

2.2.1 Nature of Cultural Patterns

Cultural patterns are of importance because they affect our behaviors and communications. They are like icebergs under water. They are in our minds. The characteristics of cultural patterns are invisible, unique and universal. They are shared or understood by members of a particular group.

Cultural patterns provide the basic set of standards that guide thought and action. Cultural patterns create the filter through which all verbal and nonverbal symbols are interpreted. Cultural patterns are primarily inside people in their mind. They provide a way of thinking about the world, of orienting oneself to it. Cultural patterns are like colored glasses that color everything people see and to which they respond. The episodes that are used to structure people's lives — attending classes, eating dinners, playing with a friend, going to work, talking with a salesperson — are certainly common to many cultures. But the interpretations that are **imposed** on these behaviors vary greatly, depending on the cultural patterns that serve as the **lens** through which the social episodes are viewed.

To sum up, cultural patterns are shared among a group of people, and they form the foundation for maintenance of cultures. They are stable over relatively long period of time, and they lead most members of a culture to behave in roughly similar ways when they encounter similar situations. Cultural patterns shape the mental programming of its people. When people study the approaches to cultural patterns, they should make some judgments about how their own cultures fit into the patterns. They should try to recognize how they, as an individual, fit into the patterns described.

2.2.2 Components of Cultural Patterns

The following are brief descriptions of the nature of the beliefs, values, norms, and social practices, which together constitute the components of cultural patterns.

2.2.2.1 Beliefs

Beliefs are ideas that people assume to be true about the world. Beliefs, therefore, are a set of learned interpretations that form the basis for cultural members to decide what is and what is not logical and correct.

Beliefs can range from ideas that are central to a person's sense of self to those that are more **peripheral**. Central beliefs include the culture's fundamental teachings about what reality is and expectations about how the world works. Less central, but also important, are beliefs derived from the teachings of those who are regarded as authorities. Parents, teachers, and other important elders transmit the cultural assumptions about the nature of the physical and interpersonal world. Peripheral beliefs refer to matters of personal taste. They contribute to each person's unique **configuration** of ideas and expectations within the larger cultural context.

Culturally shared beliefs are so fundamental to assumptions about what the world is like and how the world operates that they are typically unnoticed. What we consider to be the important "givens" about the world, such as the nature of people and their relationships with one another, are based on our culturally shared beliefs, which has been transmitted to and learned by us.

2.2.2.2 Values

Values are one's principles or standards, one's judgments of what is valuable or important in life. Values involve what a culture regards as good or bad, right or wrong, fair or unfair, just or unjust, beautiful or ugly, clean or dirty, valuable or worthless, appropriate or inappropriate, and kind or cruel. Thus, values serve as guiding principles in people's lives.

From culture to culture, values differ in their **valence** and **intensity**. Valence refers to whether the value is seen as positive or negative. Intensity indicates the strength or importance of the value, or the degree to which the culture identifies the value as significant. For example, in some American cultures, the value of respect for elders is negatively valenced and held with a modest degree of intensity. Many Americans value youth rather than oldness. In Korea, Japan, China and Mexico, however, respect for elders is a positively valenced value, and is very intensely held.

2.2.2.3 Norms

Norms are the socially shared expectations of appropriate behaviors. When a person's behaviors violate the culture's norms, social sanctions are usually imposed. Like values, norms can vary within a culture in terms of their importance and intensity. Unlike values, norms, however, may change over a period of time, whereas beliefs and values tend to be much more enduring.

Norms exist in a wide variety of behaviors of a given group of people. For example, the greeting behaviors of people within a culture are governed by norms. Similarly, good manners in a variety of situations are based on norms. Norms also exist to guide people's interactions and to indicate how to engage in conversation, what to talk about, and how to disengage from conversation. People are expected to behave according to their culture's norms, they therefore come to see their own norms as constituting the "right" way of communicating. Norms, then, are linked to the beliefs and values of a culture.

2. 2. 2. 4 Social Practices

Social practices are the predictable behavior patterns that members of a culture typically follow. Social practices are the outward manifestations of beliefs, values, and norms. For example, gifts brought by dinner guests are usually opened in the presence of the guests in the United States. In Malaysia, gifts are never opened in front of the giver, and doing so is considered bad manners.

Some social practices are informal. They include everyday behaviors such as eating, sleeping, dressing, working, playing, and talking to others. Such behaviors are so predictable and commonplace within a culture that the subtle details about how they are accomplished may pass nearly being unnoticed. For instance, **slurping** one's food in Saudi Arabia and in many Asian cultures is the usual practice, and it is regarded favorably as an expression of satisfaction and appreciation for the cooking. However, European Americans typically consider such sounds to be inappropriate.

Some other social practices are formal and prescriptive. These practices include the **rituals**, ceremonies, and structured routines that are typically performed publicly and collectively: saluting the flag, praying in church, honoring the dead at funerals, getting married, and many other social practices. Of course, all members of a culture do not necessarily follow that culture's "typical" social practices; each person differs, in unique and significant ways, from the general cultural tendency to think and behave in particular ways.

2.3 Five Cultural Orientations

Florence Kluckhohn and Fred Strodtbeck (1960) described five cultural orientations that each culture must address:

◇ What is the human orientation to activity?

◇ What is the relationship of humans to each other?

◇ What is the nature of human beings?

◇ What is the relationship of humans to the natural world?

◇ What is the orientation of humans to time?

Each culture, in its own unique way, must provide answers to these five questions in order to develop a coherent and consistent interpretation of the world. A culture's orientation to the importance and value of activity can range from passive acceptance of the world (a "being" orientation), a preference for a gradual transformation of the human condition (a "being-in-becoming" orientation), to more direct **intervention** (a "doing" orientation). A culture's solution to how it should organize itself to deal with interpersonal relationships can vary along a continuum from **hierarchical** social organization ("**linearity**") to group identification ("collectivism), and to individual autonomy ("individualism"). The available alternatives to the problem "What is the nature of human beings?" can range from "Humans are evil", to "Humans are a mixture of good and evil", and to "Humans are good." A culture's response to the preferred relationship of humans to the natural world can range from a belief that "People are **subjugated** by nature", to "People live in harmony with nature", and to "People master nature." Finally, the culture's preferred time orientation can emphasize events and experiences from the past, the present, or the future. Table 2.1 summarizes the Kluckhohn and Strodtbeck value orientation theory.

Table 2.1 Kluckhohn and Strodtbeck's Cultural Orientations

Orientation	Postulated Range of variations		
Activity	Being	Being-in-becoming	Doing
Relationships	Linearity	Collectivism	Individualism

To be continued

Orientation	Postulated Range of variations		
Human vs. nature	Good	Mixture of good and evil	Evil
People vs. nature	Subjugation to nature	Harmony with nature	Mastery over nature
Time	Past	Present	Future

(*Adapted from Florence R. Kluckhohn and Fred Strodtbeck, Variations in Value Orientation Evanston, IL: Row, Peterson, 1960*)

The five major orientations in Kluckhohn and Strodtbeck's description of cultural patterns address the manner in which a culture orients itself to activities, social relations, the self, the world, and the passage of time. There are strong linkages among the various orientations.

2.3.1 Activity Orientation

An activity orientation defines how the people of a culture view human actions and the expression of self through activities.

To define the activity orientation, cultures usually choose a point on the being-becoming-doing continuum. "Being" is an activity orientation that values inaction and acceptance of the status quo. African American and Greek cultures are usually regarded as "being" cultures. Another characterization of this orientation is a belief that all events are determined by fate and are therefore inevitable. Hindus from India often adopt this view.

A "becoming" orientation sees humans as evolving and changing. People with this orientation, including native Americans, some Asian people such as Chinese and South Koreans, are **predisposed** to think of ways to change themselves as a means of changing the world.

"Doing" is the dominant characteristic of European Americans. European Americans often ask, "What do you do?" When they first meet someone, a common greeting is "Hi! How are you doing?" and Monday morning conversations between coworkers often centre on what each person "did" over the weekend. Young people are asked what they want to be when they grow up. The "doing" cultures is often the striving culture, in which people seek to change and control what is happening to them. The common **motto** "Where there's a will there's a way" captures the essence of this cultural pattern. When faced with problems, people of "doing" cultural orientation would encourage each other to work hard, to fight on, and not give up.

How a person measures success is also related to the activity orientation. In cultures with a "doing" orientation, activity is evaluated by evaluating some observable action directed at others. Activity should have a purpose or a goal. The preferred way of dealing with a problem is to see it as a challenge. The world is viewed as something that ought to be changed in order to embody their ability and value. In the "being" and "becoming" cultures, activity is not necessarily connected to external products or actions; the great thinker is most valued.

In "doing" cultures, work is seen as a separate activity from play and an end in itself. In the "being" and "becoming" cultures, there is no clear-cut separation between work and play. For these individuals, social life spills over into their work life. When members of a "being" culture work in the environment of a "doing" culture, their behaviors are often misinterpreted. A Latin or an Asian employee might spend much work time on the telephone with family and friends. In a "doing" culture, employees who spend too much time chatting with their fellow employees may be punished by a supervisor. In the "being" and "becoming" cultures, It is common to see the employees mix working and socializing, and the employers would not punish them.

In every culture, these preferences for particular orientations to activities shape the interpersonal communication patterns. In "doing" cultures, interpersonal communication is characterized by being concerned about what people do and how they solve problems. In "being" cultures, interpersonal communication is characterized by being together rather than by accomplishing specific tasks.

2.3.2 Social Relations Orientation

The social relations orientation describes how people in a culture organize themselves and relate to each other. A social relations orientation can range from one that emphasizes differences and social hierarchy to one that strives for equality and the absence of hierarchy. Americans, for example, emphasize equality and evenness in their interpersonal relationships, even though certain groups have been treated in discriminatory and unequal ways. Equality as a value and belief is frequently expressed and is called on to justify people's actions. The phrase "We are all human, aren't we?" captures the essence of this cultural orientation. Conversely, other cultures, such as the Korean, emphasize status differences between individuals.

One noticeable difference in social relations is the degree of importance a culture places on formality. In cultures that emphasize formality, people address others by appropriate titles, and highly prescriptive rules govern the interaction. Conversely, in cultures that stress equality, people believe that human relationships develop best when those involved can be informal with one another. In America and Canada, it is acceptable that students call the first names of their professors. Students may disagree with and challenge their professors in class.

In countries such as China, Japan, and Korea, individuals identify with only a few distinct groups, and the ties that bind people to these groups are so strong that group membership may endure for a lifetime. Examples of these relationships include nuclear and extended families, friends, neighbors, work groups, and social organizations. As to Americans, friends are important for brief period of time, often serving a transitory purpose. In addition, it is accepted and even expected that European Americans often change jobs and companies or move to other places.

Another important way in which social relations orientation can vary is how people define their social roles or their position in a culture. In some cultures, family backgrounds determine a person's social position. In other countries, people, regardless of family backgrounds, can achieve success and high status. For example, Abraham Lincoln was a poor boy who went from a log cabin to the White House. A lot of American novels describe rags-to-riches stories that are achieved through hard work and perseverance.

A culture's social relations orientation affects the style of interpersonal communication. Cultures may emphasize indirectness and **ambiguity**, which is

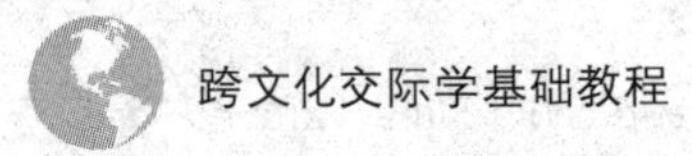

the typical pattern for Asian cultures and Eastern European cultures. The European Americans' preference for "putting your cards on the table" and "telling it like it is" reveal that they like to establish explicit, direct, and specific personal reactions, even at the expense of social discomfort on the part of the person with whom they are interacting.

2.3.3 Self-Orientation

Self-orientation describes how people's identities are formed, whether the cultural views of the self as changeable, what motivates individual actions, and the kinds of people who are valued and respected.

For most European Americans, the emphasis on the individual self is strong and pervasive. They believe the self is located solely within the individual, and the individual is definitely separate from others. From a very young age, children are encouraged to make their own decisions.

The source of motivation for human being is a part of a culture's self-orientation. Most Americans are motivated to achieve success in the form of possessions, positions, and power. Self-orientation combines with the "doing" orientation to create a set of beliefs and values that place individuals in total control of their own fate. Individuals must set their own goals and identify the means necessary to achieve them. Consequently, failure is viewed as a lack of will power and a disinclination to give the fullest efforts.

One distinguishing feature of the cultural definition of self is whether the members of the culture believe that people are inherently bad, good, or some combination of these two. The Chinese, for example, believe people are inherently good, and they must therefore be protected from exposure to corrupting influences. Conversely, other cultures such as European Americans are influenced by religious beliefs that regard humans as **intrinsically** bad.

Another additional part of self-orientation is the set of characteristics of those individuals who vary in their attitudes to the old or to the young. People in the countries such as Korea, Japan, and China respect elders and view them as a source of wisdom and valuable life experiences. They base decisions on the preferences and desires of their elders. The value on youth typifies the European American culture, in which innovation and new ideas, rather than the wisdom of the past, are regarded as important. European Americans respect the innovator and the people who try something new.

2.3.4 World Orientation

Worldview is the set of systematized beliefs and values by which a cultural group evaluates and attaches meaning to the surrounding reality (Gudykunst, 1984). Worldview is a culture's orientation toward God, humanity, nature, questions of existence, the universe and cosmos, life, death, sickness, and other philosophical issues that influence how its members perceive their world.

The central question concerning worldview is the perception of the universe. Is the universe created by a divine power? What is man's position in the universe? What is man's relationship with nature? There are usually two types of relations between humans and nature: mastery over nature and harmony with nature.

2.3.4.1 Dividedness Between Man and Nature

Western people believe that the universe is created and controlled by a divine power. Man and the universe are separated entities. The western experience of human life being separate from nature can be found in the Bible story of creation. When God created Adam, Adam was given dominance over all of God's creation. Adam and his human descendents stood apart from and above nature and were told to use the natural world to meet human needs. Western people hold firmly the belief that there are laws of nature that must be followed. With such a view of the universe, people in the west have developed a dualistic world view. They see man and the world separately, and consider that it is man's task to discover the truth established by the supernatural creator. They believe that all natural forces can be overcome and put to use by humans. The spiritual and physical worlds can be viewed as distinct. They believe that there is generally a clear understanding that the physical world, of which humans are a part, is separate from the spiritual world.

The conquest of natural conditions is the dominant assumption in the United States. The American's relationship with nature is called a "master-slave" relationship. The American mode of living, for example, is characterized by confrontation with the exploitation of the external world. They believe humans should be encouraged to control nature and exploit it. To master the natural world, people need to study and exploit it to figure out how it works. This attitude of looking at the natural world as an object has contributed to the development of Western science. Examples of this cultural belief can be found in news reports whenever a natural disaster occurs in the United States. For instance, when Hurricane Katrina hit New Orleans and elsewhere along the Gulf Coast in August 2005 and nearly two thousand people died in the subsequent flooding, people were outraged that the flood protection and levee systems could be so unsafe. The assumption in these pronouncements was that the consequences of natural forces such as hurricanes could have been prevented simply by using better technology and by reinforcing the dams and other structures to withstand the forces of nature.

2.3.4.2 Oneness Between Man and Nature

Many Asian countries such as China, Japan, and Korea hold the harmony-with-nature orientation. People in these countries draw no distinctions among human life, nature, and the supernatural — any one is just an extension of another (Kluckhohn & Strodtbeck, 1960). People live in harmony with nature.

According to old Chinese concept of universe and attitude toward nature, nature and man is one. Oneness refers to the obedience and worship of people to laws of nature. People combine the coming and going of day and night with their behavior of life. They think everything goes in a cycle. The cycle keeps going routinely. Man deals with nature harmoniously.

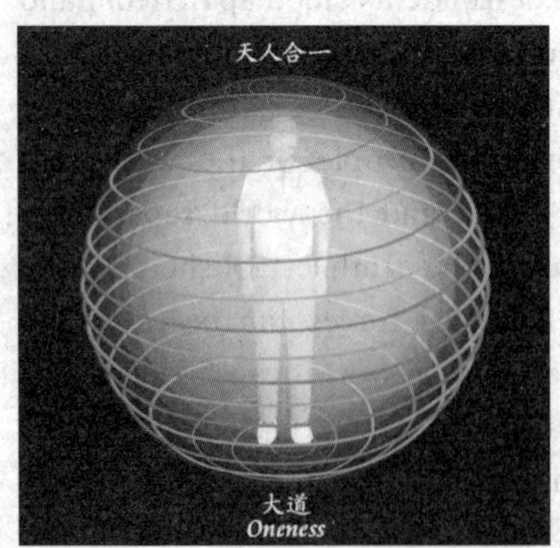

Figure 2.1 Oneness

The ancient Chinese philosophers emphasized the "one", the "blending" and the "harmony". The concept of *Tao* holds that the *One* reality is all men, gods and things: complete, all-embracing and the whole; it is an all-embracing unity from which nothing can be separated. The ancient Chinese **proposition** "*Tao* consists of *Yin* and *Yang*" initiated the notion of *Tao*. Lao Tzu, who lived 500 years before Christ, developed this concept. He said, "*Tao* gave birth to the *One*, the *One* gave birth successively to two things, three things, up to ten thousand. These ten thousand creatures cannot turn their backs to the shade (*Yin*) without having the sun (*Yang*) on their bellies, and it is on this blending of the breaths (both *Yin* and *Yang*) that their harmony depends."

Figure 2.2 Yin and Yang
Source: http://image.baidu.com

In the above picture, the *yin* and *yang* are two forces through whose essences, according to Taoist cosmology, the universe is produced and the cosmic harmony is maintained. *Yin* (the feminine and dark and passive) alternates with *yang* (the masculine and light and active). Indeed *yin* and *yang* only exist because of each other, and when the world is in a *yin* state, this is a sure sign that it is about to be in a *yang* state. The sign of the *Tao*, which means "*the Way*" to exist with nature and humans, consists of two forces in the form of a white and a black swirl. The black swirl contains a white dot and the white swirl contains a black dot. And the truest *yang* is the *yang* that is in the *yin*. The principle of *yin-yang* is the expression of the relationship that exists between opposing but interpenetrating forces that may complete one another, make each comprehensible, or create the conditions for altering one into the other.

2.3.5 Time Orientation

Time orientation concerns how people conceptualize time. Life on earth evolves in response to the cycles of day and night and the ebb and flow of the tides. As human evolves, a multiplicity of internal biological clocks also develops. These biological clocks regulate most of the physiological functions of human beings. It is not surprising; therefore, human concepts of time grow out of natural association with daily, monthly, and annual cycles. Time orientation is another factor that distinguishes cultures.

A culture's time orientation suggests the pace of life. The fast pace of European Americans, governed by clocks, appointments, and schedules, has become commonly accepted. They view time as a scarce and valuable commodity similar to money or other economic investments. They strive to "save time," "make time," "spend time," and "gain time." Events during a day are dictated by a schedule of activities, precisely defined and differentiated.

On the contrary, the pace of life in countries such as India, Kenya, and Argentina is more relaxed and comfortably paced. People in these cultures bring an entirely different orientation to time. They do not define punctuality as precisely as European Americans do. Thus, time is viewed as ongoing and endless.

Time is an element we all know but often overlook. Although we cannot hold or see time, we respond to it as if it had command over our lives. Because time is such a personal phenomenon, all of us perceive and treat it in a manner that expresses our character.

New Words and Phrases

anthropological /ˌænθrəpəˈlɒdʒɪkəl/ *adj*. 人类学的
dynamic /daɪˈnæmɪk/ *adj*. 动态的，动力的，有活力的
impose /ɪmˈpəʊz/ *vt*. 强加
lens /lenz/ *n*. 透镜，镜头
peripheral /pəˈrɪfərəl/ *adj*. 不重要的，外围的
configuration /kənˌfɪgjʊˈreɪʃən/ *n*. 结构
valence /ˈveɪləns/ *n*. 化合价，效价
intensity /ɪnˈtensɪti/ *n*. 强度，能量
slurp /slɜːp/ *n*. 啜食声 *v*. 出声地吃
ritual /ˈrɪtjʊəl/ *n*. 宗教仪式，典礼 *adj*. 仪式的
orientation /ˌɔːrɪenˈteɪʃən/ *n*. 信仰，定位，导向

intervention /ɪntəˈvenʃən/ *n*. 介入
hierarchical /ˌhaɪəˈrɑːkɪkl/ *adj*. 按等级划分的
linearity /ˌlɪnɪˈærɪti/ *n*. 直线性
subjugate /ˈsʌbdʒʊget/ *vt*. 征服,使服从,抑制
predispose /ˌpriːdɪsˈpəʊz/ *v*. (使)预先偏向于
motto /ˈmɒtəʊ/ *n*. 格言;箴言
ambiguity /ˈæmbɪˈgjuːɪti/ *n*. 含糊不清
intrinsically /ɪnˈtrɪnsɪkəli/ *adv*. 内在地,固有地
proposition /ˌprɒpəˈzɪʃən/ *n*. 命题;主张
condition /kənˈdɪʃən/ *vt*. 制约 *vt*. & *vi*. 对……具有重要影响

Exercises

I. Questions for discussion

1. Edward T. Hall says, "There is not one aspect of human life that is not touched and altered by culture." Do you agree with Hall? If so, why?
2. Do you believe that you have your own unique identities that separate you from others? What are your unique identities?
3. How do you think each of the five cultural patterns is displayed in Chinese culture?
4. Talk about how cultural patterns decide your communicative styles.
5. Give examples to illustrate the time orientation you hold in daily life.

II. Multiple choice

Directions: Choose the best answer to each of the following questions.

1. Any change in the subsystem of culture will affect the whole system indicates ________.
   A. Culture is holistic　　B. Culture is shared
   C. Culture is created　　D. Culture is learned
2. Phrases like "make time", "save time" and "gain time" indicate people's ________ time orientation.
   A. past-oriented　　B. present-oriented
   C. future-oriented　　D. none of them
3. Hegel said, "When man feels he is limitless at the sea, he will have great

courage to surpass the limit." This quotation indicates ________.

A. unity of man and nature　　B. world view

C. social relation orientation　　D. future-oriented time orientation

4. Norms are the ________ behavior patterns for the members of a social system.

A. temporary　　B. past

C. established　　D. future

5. People who hold a dualistic world view believe ________.

A. man and nature are separate.

B. all natural forces can be overcome and put to use by humans.

C. man can conquer nature.

D. Man is one part of nature.

III. Fill in the blanks with the words given in the bank

education	material	context	society	referent
agriculture	refer	usage	referent	agriculture

In current usage, culture includes language, beliefs, customs, institutions, and physical objects, etc. Shortly, culture is the large-scale __(1)__ of a given society.

When culture first began to take its current __(2)__ by Europeans in the 18th and 19th centuries, it connoted a process of __(3)__ or improvement, as in __(4)__ or horticulture. In the 19th century, it came to __(5)__ first to the betterment or refinement of the individual, especially through __(6)__, and then to the fulfillment of national aspirations or ideals. In the mid-19th century, some scientists used the term "culture" to refer to a universal human capacity. In the 20th century, "culture" emerged as a concept central to __(7)__, encompassing all human phenomena that are not purely results of human genetics. A distinction is current between the physical artifacts created by a __(8)__, its so-called __(9)__ culture and everything else, the intangibles such as language, customs, etc. that are the main __(10)__ of the term "culture".

Case I

Tom, an exchange student from England, is talking with Mary, his girlfriend from Australia in Tom's dorm room about their holidays. At this time, Yahan, an exchange student from India, enters in the room unannounced.

Tom: (to Mary) So, I think we should spend a week in China, 4 days in Japan. It is fantastic to know the East.

(Yahan enters)

Yahan: Hello Tom. Who is this with you?

Tom: Oh, hi Yahan. This is Mary. Mary, this is Yahan; he lives just down the hall.

Mary: Hi Yahan.

Yahan: Is this your girlfriend, Tom?

Tom: Ah ... yeah, she is.

Yahan: Are you two going to marry? Want children?

Tom: Ah, well ....

Mary: Uh ... we really haven't discussed that yet.

Yahan: Oh, I see. Is your family not wealthy enough for her, Tom? What is your father's occupation?

Tom: What?

Questions for Discussion

1. Why didn't Tom give direct answers to Yahan's questions?
2. Did Yahan intend to intrude Tom's privacy?
3. What cultural differences does this case reveal?

Case Analysis

Indians tend to initiate social conversations with strangers easily. They often ask, without embarrassment, very personal and delicate questions concerning one's age, marital status, income, occupation, religious beliefs, and so on. Some of their questions are considered to be an intrusion of one's privacy to westerners. Westerners need to learn that these questions are not to be taken with any offense.

In the above case, Tom and Mary are from the western cultures. They value privacy. When Yahan asks questions concerning personal relationships, marriage, and even Tom's father's occupation, they think it hard for them to answer. The case shows misunderstanding and embarrassing situations caused by cultural differences in intercultural communication.

Case II

Kenneth, an American student, met Vernon, a student recently arrived from Malaysia, and they decided to have dinner together at the university cafeteria. In the cafeteria, Kenneth ordered a pizza and some other food for their dinner. When the food was sent to them, Kenneth tore the pizza into pieces and handed one piece to Vernon, using his left hand. Vernon took that piece of pizza and put it on his plate without eating it. Kenneth was quite confused about what had gone wrong, so he asked Vernon, "Are you all right?" "Yes, I'm fine," Vernon replied. Kenneth kept on asking, "Why don't you eat the pizza?" Vernon said nothing but began to eat the other food, ignoring the pizza. Kenneth was confused but he ceased his questioning. And the two just kept on eating without much conversation.

Questions for Discussion

1. How would you explain Vernon's behavior?
2. Give an example to describe religious beliefs in your cultures that might cause misunderstanding in intercultural communication.
3. What cultural implication does this case reveal?

Case Analysis

In Malaysia, most people believe in Islam. Malayan believe that their right hands are clean and left hands are dirty. They would use their right hands to pass objects instead of left hands. In the daily life, usually there is no toilet paper in the washing rooms. Malayan are used to using their right hand to hold a water pipe and using their left hand to wash their butts.

In this case, Kenneth has no knowledge of Islam. His behavior of taking a piece of pizza by using his left hand is against Malayan taboo. Vernon, as a

Malayan, would not eat any food taken with other's left hand. To maintain his relations with Kenneth or not to make Kenneth embarrassed, he does not tell the reasons directly but put the pizza on the plate. It is certain that their misunderstanding is caused by cultural differences.

Further Reading

Reading I

On Culture

Culture is defined as "everything that people have, think, and do as members of a society." The definition covers all of the three components of culture: material objects, belief systems and behavior patterns. According to Ferraro, everything that people think refers to what people have in mind, such as ideas, values and attitudes; what people have refers to the material possessions; and what people do refers to their behavior patterns. As members of a society suggests that the sharing of the three components is the passport of one's admittance into a society.

Culture is like an iceberg

Culture is often said to be like an iceberg. Surface culture, the part above the waterline, is composed of tangible things such as food, dresses, languages, architecture, music, art and nonverbal cues. The major part of culture, however, is beneath the surface and primarily out of our awareness. It is made up of hidden realities including perceptions, beliefs, values, assumptions, expectations, tastes and preferences.

Figure 2.3 an iceberg picture

Hall (1959) pointed out that culture hides more than it reveals, and strangely

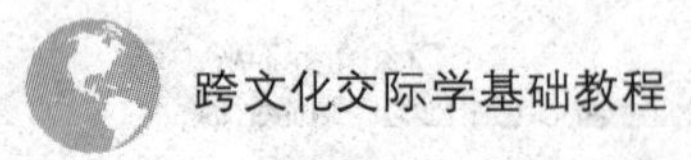

enough what it hides, it hides most effectively from its own participants. Some of culture is visible. Aspects of culture that we can easily observe are often referred to as objective culture. This culture includes things such as history, literature, and customs. Most of culture is below the surface of our awareness. It is referred to as subjective culture. It includes feelings and attitudes about how things are and how they should be.

When people talk about culture, they usually mean some aspects of the objective culture, that is the part of the iceberg seen above the water. However, we should focus on the awareness of the hidden part of the iceberg.

Culture is our software

Culture is the basic operating system that makes us human. Human around the world are physically pretty much the same. There are variations in body size, shape and color, but the basic equipment is universal. We can think of our physical selves as the hardware, but we cannot be said to be human until we are programmed and each of us is programmed by our home culture. At birth the infant is only a potential human. It must learn how to be human and it learns that in a culturally specific way. It is the culture that forms the software.

Culture is the software of the mind. Think of the human mind as a computer where information is entered, stored, and recalled. For example, as we sit at our computer, we type in information (i.e. data input). After a while, we decide to take a break from writing and we press the save button, which stores the information in the computer's memory. Later, when we return to the computer, we recall the information (i.e. open the saved file) and continue writing. The human mind works in the same way. Via our senses, we take in memory, and later we recall it. All human brains, regardless of culture, take in, store, and recall information. Such processes are necessary for communication. Without the ability to take in, store, and recall information, human communication would be impossible. Culture represents the computer's (i.e. the brain's) software. In other words, how we take in information, how we store it, and how we recall it, are all based on our culture, that is, our software.

Culture is the grammar of our behavior

Culture is what people need to know in order to behave appropriately in any society. It includes all the rules that make actions meaningful to those acting and to the people around them. In learning to speak, we learn to use the grammar of our native language, but we use it automatically with little or even no conscious awareness of the rules of grammar. Similarly we learn our cultural grammar unconsciously and apply its rules automatically. Just as native speakers of a language are usually unable to describe the grammatical rules of that language unless they have specifically studied grammar, most people find it difficult to describe the meaning system of their own culture.

We should add new software to the basic operating systems. This means acquiring new cultural skills. It is possible and advisable to add additional software to our operating system to increase its power and flexibility. We would like to add cultural software in order to be successful and comfortable in the global village. Just as we need to know more than one language, we need to know more than one cultural grammar.

To do these we need to look at our own culture as a system of meaning, as a grammar of our experience and behavior. We need to become a software engineer who can figure out how our own operating system works. Once we do that, it is possible to add some new programming. Using another image, we need to become aware of the water we are swimming in like a fish. With greater awareness of our own culture, we will better understand the meaning system of other cultures and will be better able to adapt to them.

Reading II

Eastern and Western Cultures and Relationships

As demonstrated by Gudykunst and Nishida (1986), perceptions of relationships differ widely across cultures. In individualistic cultures such as the United States, relationships are typically viewed from the perceptive of the self. Individuals see themselves as distinct individuals who participate in relationships to maximize their own self-interests. In many collectivistic cultures, like China, relationships are guided by Confucianism. The fundamental theme of Confucianism is that proper relationships form the cornerstone of society. Moreover, an individual's conduct in society should be guided by four principles: ⓐ *humanism*: treating others as one wishes to be treated; ⓑ *faithfulness*: loyalty rather than personal interest or profit; ⓒ ***propriety***（礼节，礼仪）: social **decorum**（礼节，礼仪）and **etiquette**（礼节，礼仪）; and ⓓ *wisdom*.

Many people in Eastern cultures hold the belief that there are particular or unique rules and guidelines that apply to each individual relationship. Relational partners are to be sensitive to differences in such things as status when interacting with others. They believe in strict and well-defined social hierarchies in which people are perceived as higher or lower. In contrast, persons in Western cultures try to treat others as equally as possible, regardless of status or intimacy level of the partners.

Relational partners in Eastern cultures engage in long-term and **asymmetrical**（非对称的，不均匀的）**reciprocity**（相互性，互惠主义）. Reciprocity refers to the give-and-take or mutual exchange in interpersonal encounters. In Confucian philosophy, dependency on others is an inevitable and accepted part of relations with others. People will always be **indebted**（使负债）to others who help them in some way. People do not calculate what they give and receive. To calculate would be to think about immediate personal profits, which is the opposite of the principle of faithfulness. Western relationships, on the other hand, are characterized by short-term and **symmetrical**（匀称的，对称的）reciprocity or even contractual reciprocity. In the United States, for example, some marital relationships begin with premarital legal agreements that carefully spell out expectations, possessions, and obligations that are to be followed.

In many Eastern cultures, there is a clear difference between who is or is not a member of the ingroups or the outgroups. Confucian philosophy prescribes that people associate and identify with relatively few, yet very cohesive groups. Moreover, one's **affiliation**（友好关系；联盟）with ingroups is long-lived, perhaps even lifelong. Group associations in most Western cultures are, for the most part, optional and voluntary. Many of the groups with whom one associates in the United States, for example, are designed to somehow facilitate one's individual development, and one's association with the group lasts only as long as one benefits from membership.

A fourth difference between relationships in Eastern and Western cultures is the use of intermediaries (go-betweens). For the most part, persons in Western cultures prefer direct, face-to-face contact in interpersonal relationships, including with business associates. In the United States, for example, the use of **intermediary** (仲裁者，调解者) is typically reserved for very formal or legal situations and is usually contractual (as with lawyers). In Eastern cultures, because the distinctions between ingroups and outgroups are so well defined, intermediaries are essential and are used even in informal situations, such as introductions, dating, and marital arrangements, and relatively small business transactions. The principle behind the use of intermediaries is to save face.

A fifth difference in interpersonal relations in Eastern and Western cultures is that Confucianism's emphasis on faithfulness and loyalty in relationships leads to blending of personal and public relationships. Many Eastern cultures prefer to do business with trusted associates with whom they have established a strong interpersonal bond. In the United States, people can maintain "strict business" relationships. Many U.S. businesses would be well served by initiating frequent contact, establishing mutual interests, and developing shared experiences with their Eastern culture counterparts.

Adapted from Intercultural Communication — A Contextual Approach by James W. Neuliep, 1957.

Chapter Three

Three Core Cultural Dimensions

- **Objectives**
- Understand nature of value.
- Understand individualism and collectivism.
- Understand nature of context.
- Understand high-context and low-context communication.
- Understand monochronic and polychromic time orientation.

导读

价值观、语境和时间观是影响跨文化交际的三个最为核心的文化维度。价值观是人们对周围的客观事物(包括人、事、物)的意义、重要性的总评价和总看法。Hofstede 提出的个人主义—集体主义价值观理论对了解东西方文化差异具有重要意义。个人主义强调个人权利和个人选择的优先性,集体主义则把集体的利益放到第一位。

语境是使用语言的环境,包括一切主、客观因素。美国人类学家霍尔 1976 年根据文化与语境之间不同程度的联系,将世界文化抽象分为从高语境到低语境的文化连续流。在高语境文化中,说话者的言语或行为意义来源于或内在化于说话者当时所处的语境。在低语境文化中,人们强调的是双方交流的内容,而不是当时所处的语境。他的高低语境理论概括并诠释了不同文化群体所表现出的交际风格的显著差异。

时间观是人们对时间概念的科学认识或哲学认识。霍尔把不同文化的时间分为两种范畴，即单向计时制和多向计时制。前者是一种强调日程、期限、效率，在一个时间里做一件事情的时间习惯。而后者讲究时间使用的灵活性，倾向于一个时间里做多种事情的时间习惯。时间取向和时间的使用反映了不同文化群体人们的价值观及交际风格的差异。

Text

3.1 Values

Value is "a conception, **explicit** or **implicit**, distinctive of an individual or characteristic of a group, of the desirable which influences the selection from available modes, means, and ends of action" (Kluckhohn, 1951). Values form the basic lenses through which we view our own actions and actions of others. They set the background criteria for how we should communicate appropriately with others. They also set the emotional tone for how we interpret and evaluate cultural strangers' behaviors.

3.1.1 Nature of Values

Concise Oxford Dictionary defines **values** as "*one's principles or standards, one's judgment of what is valuable or important in life.*" Values set norms, shape beliefs, and underline and regulate attitudes. Values vary in ethnic, regional and national layers. **Filial piety** is a critical value in China, while it is less likely to matter most to Americans.

Values fundamentally influence our behavior in society. They do not describe how we act in a culture but dictate what we ought or ought not to do. Values tend to be the basis of all the decisions we make and provide standards for us to evaluate our own and others' behaviors (Guo-ming Chen, William J. Starosta, 2007).

According to Hofstede(2008), values can not be measured by scientists,

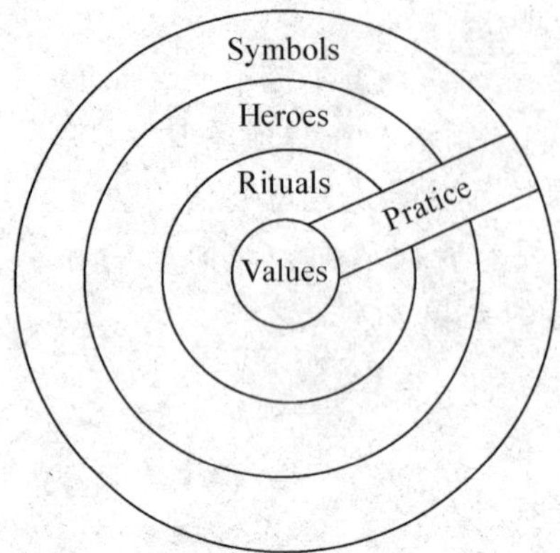

Figure 3.1 The "Onion Diagram": Manifestations of Culture at Different Levels of Depth

because they are not accessible to clinical experimentation. People are accustomed to use the "Onion Diagram" as a metaphor to describe values. Being the innermost "skin of the onion", values lie at the core of a culture. They are invisible until they become evident in practices, which are pictured as the "layers of onion" around the core that consists of values.

In the above "Onion Diagram", symbols, heroes and rituals constitute practice. Symbols, such as clothes, languages, architectures, lie at the outer layers that are visible by eyes. Heroes are put next to symbols. The personalities of the respected heroes are typical representatives for the majority of people in one culture. In other words, understanding heroes' personalities, to a very high extent, helps deepen the understanding of people in the same culture. The third layer is rituals, which are unique expressions of people's behavior in one culture. For instance, Chinese people usually sit down in different places depending on their importance when they are eating. Japanese bow to each other when they meet and they usually take off shoes before stepping into a room. Values are displayed in the inner layer. They set criteria for all the elements in practice.

Core values seldom change although customs, practice, rituals and other behaviors might change. In order to understand cultural values, people can keenly observe and measure the manifested "layers" people practice. In addition, a value can not be isolated from the overall value system of a culture. It is significant to study values and value orientations because of their stability in feature and the guidance to people's behaviors.

3.1.2 Individualism & Collectivism

The dimension of **individualism-collectivism** refers to the relationship one perceives between one's self and the group of which one is a member.

Individualism demonstrates the following cultural tendency: ① the individual being the most important single unit in any social setting, ② independence rather than dependence, ③ individual achievement, and ④ the uniqueness of each individual.

Collectivism reveals people lay great emphasis on ① the views, needs and goals of the in-groups rather than oneself; ② social norms and duty defined by the in-group rather than one's behavior to get pleasure; ③ beliefs shared with the in-group rather than beliefs that distinguish self from the in-group; and ④ great readiness to cooperate with in-group members.

Hofstede (1983, 1984) initially surveyed more than 100,000 IBM employees in seventy-one countries. Throughout theoretical reasoning and statistical analysis, he provides an excellent synthesis of the relationships between cultural values and social behaviors. Hofstede's research indicates that individualism is a cultural pattern that is found in most northern and western regions of Europe and in North America. Collectivism is a cultural pattern common in Asia, Africa, the Middle East, Central and South America, and Pacific islands. While less than one-third of the world population resides in cultures with high individualistic value tendencies, a little more than two-thirds of the people live in cultures with high collectivistic value tendencies.

Individual orientation versus collective orientation is one of the basic pattern variables that determine human behaviors. Although people habitually take individualism and collectivism as separate entities, all peoples and cultures have both individual and collective orientations.

3.1.2.1 Individualism

As one of the basic orientations of cultural values, individualism was first used by the French historian and politician Alexis de Tocqueville (1805 - 1859). Basically, individualism refers to the broad value tendencies of culture in emphasizing the importance of individual identity over group identity, individual rights over group rights, and individual needs over group needs. Individualism promotes self-efficiency, individual responsibilities, and personal autonomy.

In cultures that tend toward individualism, competition is encouraged;

personal goals take precedence over group goals; people tend not to emotionally depend on organizations and institutions; and every person has the right to his or her possessions, opinions and thoughts. These cultures focus on individual initiatives and achievements. In the United States where individualism is valued, competitiveness is encouraged as means for trying to be the best. There is a proverb in America, "The squeaky wheel gets the grease." This implies that you will receive rewards by distinguishing yourself from others; people ought to speak up and be noticed.

Individuals in individualistic cultures make career choices on the basis of personal needs and goals. They are **pragmatic** and striving in activity. If a job offers insufficient advancement, or a personality conflicts arise with a superior, or the tasks become boring, an ambitious individual likely transfers his job to another one.

To the holistic extent, people in individualistic cultures are optimistic, pragmatic, and striving in activity. They fancy making decisions independently. They are conscious of responsibility, rule of law, privacy protection. They stress objection, frankness, practicality in social communication. They prefer explicit behavioral and communicative style over implicit and **roundabout** style. They highly value time concept. It is opposite with the **conformist** Japanese's concept of "the nail that sticks up gets hammered down."

The American Values of Individualism

Individualism has affected the development of America. Benjamin Franklin described individualism in his works "God helps those who help themselves." The former Prime Minister Churchill once said, "We got our names from our parents not possessions. We must seek for opportunities. My specialty/honor comes not from my parents, but achieved by my efforts."

The liberal theme of individualism is linked to the theme of being equal — equal rights and equal opportunities. **Enshrined** in *the Declaration of Independence*, the Constitution, *the Bill of Rights*, and democratic and capitalistic institutions, the liberal principles constitute the core of the American cultural **ethos**. The pursuit of individual rights and interests is considered utterly legitimate.

Many Americans prefer to use the word "freedom" to mean what scholars call individualism. By freedom, they mean the desire and the ability of all individuals to control their own destiny without interference from the government, a ruling noble class, the church or any other organized authority. So Americans are expected to take initiative in advancing their personal interests and well-being and to be direct and assertive in interacting with others. Americans believe that individuals must learn to rely on themselves. This means achieving both financial and emotional independence from their parents as early as possible, usually by the age of 18 or 21. The American value of individualism is reflected in the belief that individuals should set their own goals and then pursue them independently. Individuals have the power to determine their own destiny.

Some scholars refer to the American culture as "I" culture. There are more than 150 words in nearly any English dictionary with affixes "self-": self-control, self-esteem, self-confidence, self-reliance, self-denial, self-respect in English dictionaries. Americans are educated to become self-made man and self-made woman when they are young. Self-actualization and the maximal realization of individual potential are supreme aims in life.

American people advocate the spirits of trying, being competitive and ambitious. American People believe that competition, as well as the desire to try and win are healthy and desirable. They take life as a race, hence they must run the race in order to succeed; they must compete with others. That is a price to be **remunerated** for the equality of opportunity. If everyone has an equal chance to succeed, then it is every person's duty to try. Americans match their energy and intelligence against that of their neighbors in a competitive contest for success. People who are more competitive and successful are honored by being called "winners". Competition is a part of life from early childhood to retirement from work. Competition is carried into schools, workplaces and daily activities. So there are such sayings as "*Every man for himself and God for us all.*" "*Every man is the architect of his own fortune.*" and "*Upward mobility*" is admired.

America is a society where people seek for more material wealth. The main reason is that material wealth is the most widely accepted measure of status there. Americans hold the belief that possessions are important in life. American economic system is dynamic and depends on the constant circulation of money to ensure full employment. The U.S. system encourages people to buy things and then to buy the "new improved" versions as new things quickly become obsolete. People are judged by their possessions: Where do they live? What kind of car does she or he drive? What does she wear to the party? The quality and quantity of an individual's material possessions become the accepted evaluation of success and social status.

In America, social relations are based on the autonomy of each person. Each person is seen as autonomous and separate. It means that each person should be treated as an individual first and only secondarily as a member of a group or occupant of a position in a hierarchy. An American would regard himself as independent body, a separate part in a machine, a man different from others. They think it a shame to rely on their parents. Each person in America has his privacy and seeks for the freedom of privacy and difference. Americans like to be different and special. They pursue individual happiness, free development, self will, self freedom, and self ambition. In America, self-reliance and independence are important, and one is considered weak to be dependent on others. Each person acts independently and is responsible for his actions. Children learn to express their individual desires and make individual choices when they are very young. The mother of a two-year-old child might ask her son what he wants for breakfast. She gives him a choice between two different breakfast cereals and two kinds of fruit juice. The child is learning to make choices and decisions and to experience his needs and desires as more important than other considerations. People are more likely to express pride in themselves and their accomplishment rather than to express pride in their group.

Americans have a special feeling about jobs, defining self and others by occupation. Work becomes part of one's identity. Many American people agree that a "feeling of accomplishment" is the most important aspect of work. Work is considered very seriously in the United States. Work is separated from play. Americans try to be best, to go ahead, and to be independent. They try to create chances instead of waiting for chances. They think their future is under their foot or in their own hands.

3. 1. 2. 2 Collectivism

Collectivism refers to the broad value tendencies of a culture in emphasizing the importance of the "we" identity over the "I" identity, group rights over individual rights, and in-group-oriented needs over individual wants and desires. Collectivism promotes relational interdependence, in-group harmony, and in-group collaborative spirit (Ting-Toomey, 1988).

A "we" consciousness prevails instead of an "I" orientation. Collectivism values the group above the individual, and individuals have a responsibility to the group that supersedes individual needs or rights. Throughout Asia, in different degrees, collectivism is celebrated. What matters is the close-knit interlocked human network. Harmony among the interdependent group members is the key, and it takes priority above nearly all other values.

A rigid social framework that distinguishes between in-groups and out-groups characterizes collectivism. People count on their in-group (relatives, clans, organizations) to look after them, and in exchange, they owe absolute loyalty to the group. People express pride, loyalty, and solidarity with their family or group. They take pride in and define their sense of self quite literally, their sense of identity among them are in terms of their family or similar group. The individual is emotionally dependent on organizations and institutions, and the culture gives emphasis of belonging to organizations. Individuals trust the group decisions even at the expense of individual rights. A well-known expression can explain the message in collectivism: "No matter how stout, one beam cannot support a house."

In collectivist society, people are **fatalistic** to activity. They stress hierarchical ranks and formality. People highly value cooperation and harmonious atmosphere, which is in line with the "face theory". Tactful and **low-key** attitudes are quite desired. Extreme behavior, even friendly aggression and conflicts in social interaction are quite undesired and embarrassing.

The Chinese Values of Collectivism

In China, people have strong honor of collectivism or group. They attach importance to the interests of family, group, community, society and country. Individual interests may be put in the second position. When people

Figure 3.2 The Opening Ceremony of the Beijing Olympics

deal with the relation between oneself and group, they are required to follow the rules and control themselves. In China, people at home are dependent on their parents. The parents not only support children's educational fees but arrange children's marriage as well. Some children even live together with their parents after they get married. At work, Chinese people depend on and try to cooperate with each other. They would first consider others' opinion before they say or do things, which indicates their concern for face. They try to fit in with others, act appropriately, promote others' goals, and seek for conformity and cooperation.

Based on Confucianism, self is relational in Chinese culture. That is, the self is defined by the surrounding relations. Traditionally, the Chinese self involves multiple layers of relationships with others. A person in this relational network tends to be sensitive to his or her position as above, below, or equal to others. The relations are often derived from kinship networks and supported by cultural values such as filial piety, loyalty, dignity, and integrity.

Holding such orientation has positive and negative points. In positive aspects, Chinese people are modest, cautious, cooperative, and diligent. They owe their honor to group, surroundings and others' help. They stress "relations" among people. This orientation leads to inner character, endurance. In negative aspects, Chinese people are lack of the spirit of forwardness, competition and ambition.

3.1.3 Individualist-Collectivist Priorities

The individualist-collectivist priorities interpret how cultures define obligation differently. Obligation has rules, determined by different cultural priorities, and that can cause problems in intercultural encounters.

Table 3.1 Priorities of Cultural Values of Individualism and Collectivism

Individualism	Collectivism	Individualism	Collectivism
1. Freedom	1. Belonging	6. Efficiency	6. Quality
2. Independence	2. Group harmony	7. Time	7. Patience
3. Self-reliance	3. Collectiveness	8. Directness	8. Indirectness
4. Equality	4. Age/Seniority	9. Openness	9. Go-between
5. Competition	5. Cooperation		

Hofstede (1980) states that, in an individualistic society, each individual is likely to seek for his/her own interest and try to maximize the gains from any opportunity that might present itself. In a collectivistic society, on the other hand, members identify with the organization and act in unison to accomplish the organization's goals. This sense of interdependence, loyalty, and joint obligation to the system would also foster a more co-operative and informal communication and co-ordination mechanism to operate in the system as the goals of the organization are being achieved.

3.1.4 Values and Communication

Values underline attitudes. They also shape beliefs. Values enable us to evaluate what matters to us or to apply standards to our attitudes and beliefs. Therefore, values definitely influence communication.

Sitaram and Haapanen (1979) summarized the relationship between values and human communication as follows:

First, values are communicated, both explicitly and implicitly, through verbal and nonverbal behavior. Although what we say or what we do may reflect our personal motives or are somewhat constrained by the context of a situation, most of our speech and actions reflect the values embedded in our mind that have been learned through the long-term socialization process.

Values are normally expressed through verbal and nonverbal behaviors. Verbal expressions are used to highlight the importance of specific values to individuals or groups. Proverbs demonstrate how verbal expressions are used to underscore values. For example, certain cultural values are expressed in the proverbs used by North Americans:

- Time and action: "*Time is money*," and "*A stitch in time saves nine*."
- Practicality: "*A bird in the hand is worth two in the bush*," "*Don't cry over the spilt milk*."
- Privacy: "*A man's home is his castle*."
- Cleanliness: "*Cleanliness is next to godliness*."
- Future orientation: "*Take care of today, and tomorrow will take care of itself*."

Nonverbally, we tend to communicate our values through social rituals. For example, the custom of frequently exchanging gifts in China and Japan reflects the cultural values of reciprocity, generosity, and friendship.

Second, the way in which people communicate is influenced by the values they hold. Communication is shaped by our value system, because values determine what is desirable and what is undesirable. For instance, harmony as a dominate Chinese culture value leads the Chinese to avoid saying "no", to speak admiringly and respectfully of each other, and to avoid expressing aggressive behaviors in social interactions.

Gudykunst and Ting-Toomey (1996) argue that individualistic values positively influence the use of dramatic communication, the use of feelings to guide behavior, openness of communication, and preciseness of communication. Collectivistic values positively influence the tendency to use indirect communication and be interpersonally sensitive. The following table shows how values influence people in behavioral traits.

Table 3.2 Behavioral Traits Associated with Individualism and Collectivism

Individualism	Collectivism
Optimism High self-esteem Lower social anxiety Emotional expression Satisfaction with self Satisfaction with freedom Ease of interacting with strangers Direct communication style Lower relational commitment Preference to work alone	Social self-concept Need for affiliation Sensitivity to rejection Sensitivity to embarrassment In-group relationship preferences Indirect communication style Valuing of social networks

To sum up, cultural values guide both perception and communication. An understanding of cultural value orientations helps people appreciate and understand the behavior of other people in different cultures. To reach understanding in intercultural communication, we should follow two rules: ① understand each other's values, and ② adjust our communication style to make it in line with each other's values. ③ respect each other's values instead of judging them.

3.2 Context

Context is a key element in both communication and culture. A communication that takes place within a setting or situation is called a context. The expectations individuals have for consequences of particular actions depend on the experiences of others woven into a particular cultural context. Context helps communicators conquer barriers in communication and achieve full understanding.

Cultural context theory is put forward by Edward Hall in his book *Beyond Culture*. He claims that meaning and context are bound up with each other. While a linguistic code can be analyzed on some levels independent of context, the code, the context, and the meaning can only be seen as different aspects of a single event. Context is the information that surrounds an event; it is inextricably bound up with the meaning of the event.

Study in context may be converted from the single high or low context to multiple contexts, and it emphasizes different situational contexts, for instance, the place where people meet, the social purpose for being together, and the nature of the relationship. Thus, context includes elements like physical, social, and interpersonal settings within which messages are exchanged.

3.2.1 Low-Context and High-Context Communication

According to Hall (1976), a **high-context** (HC) communication is one in which most of the information is either in the physical context or internalized in the person, while very little is in the coded, explicit, transmitted part of the message. A **low-context** (LC) communication is just the opposite; the mass of the information is vested in the explicit code.

Depending on the degree to which culture relates to context, the world cultures are placed in a **cultural continuum** that ranges from high-context on one end to low-context on the other end. High and low-context division is not very absolute, since each culture harbors **hybridism** (Dai Xiaodong, 2011). Contextual flexibility should not be neglected (Chen Guoming, 2012).

On the basis of the role of context in people's communication, Hall introduced an evident distinction between high-context and low-context communication based on ways of expression, attitudes towards in-group and out-group members and time orientation, which is another very important tool for examining cultural differences. Gudykunst (1988) have argued that, Hall's distinction can be considered as an aspect of collectivism versus individualism. High-context communication fits the collectivist society, and low-context communication is typical for individualist cultures.

3.2.1.1 Low-context Communication

Low-context communication refers to communication patterns of direct verbal mode — straight talk, nonverbal **immediacy** and sender-oriented values. It means that the sender assumes the responsibility to communicate directly. In low context communication, most of the information must lie in the transmitted message in order to make up for what is missing in the context. The speaker is expected to be responsible for constructing a clear, persuasive message that the listener can decode easily.

In low-context cultures, such as German and America, most of the information is contained in the verbal message, and very little is embedded in the context or within the participants. Low-context communicators would speak their minds and tell the truth and be open and precise with others. Americans call for direct and clear communication. Direct communication stresses speakers' ability to express their intentions. For example, when asking someone to close the door, an American might say in a direct and clear way "The door is open" or "Would you close the door?" Americans might use signs, instruction lists, and standard operating procedures. They often use the injunctions such as "Say what you mean," "Get to the point."

Low-context culture is a **manifest culture** — communications are highly dependent on verbal communications. Generally with Americans, what you see (or hear) is what you get, particularly in business. There is no "**beating around the bush.**" Directness is preferred over politeness and diplomacy. This may sound blunt to the Asian or European ear, used to an eloquent discourse or intellectual debate. Americans, however, prefer exchanges to be brief, clear, and precise — preferably delivered in **a sound bite**.

Similar with the communication style, the style of thinking is a linear progression through a logical sequence of facts to one clear conclusion — cause and effect, connect the dots. Americans place trust in objective, concrete facts and data. Information is conveyed in the explicit verbal message. There is no need for subtle, hidden meanings, or **extraneous** information. Written reports will be headed with a brief "executive summary" — probably written **in bullet points**.

3.2.1.2 High-context Communication

A high-context message is one in which "most of the information is either in the physical context or internalized in the person, while very little is in the coded, explicit, transmitted part of the message" (Hall, 1976). High-context communication refers to communication patterns of indirect verbal talk, and nonverbal subtleties. It means that the receiver or interpreter of the message assumes the responsibility to infer the hidden or contextual meanings of the message (Ting-Toomey, 1985). In high-context communication, the listener of interpreter of the message is expected to "read between the lines," to accurately infer the implicit intent of the verbal message, and to observe the nonverbal nuances and subtleties that accompany and enhance the verbal messages.

High-context transactions feature preprogrammed information that is in the receiver and in the setting, with only minimal information in the transmitted message. Most of the information is the physical context or is internalized in the people who are a part of the interaction. Very little information is actually coded in the verbal message. High-context communicators are not open but would like to be reserved. Asking someone to close the door, a Chinese in an indirect way might say "It is somewhat cold today" to imply that the door should be closed because of the cold weather.

By high-context communication people emphasize how intention or meaning can best be conveyed through the context (e.g., social roles or positions) and the nonverbal channels (e.g., pauses, silence, tone of voice) of the verbal message. In high-context cultures such as those of Japan, Korea, and China, people tend to be more aware of their surroundings and their environment and do not rely on verbal communication as their main information source.

Chinese prefer the use of understatement. When they communicate with others, they would talk in an indirect way. "Maybe" is often used in conversations. In Japan, extreme politeness and extreme tact are standard. Japanese people are concerned about group harmony, and a nondirective social style may be the best way to engage in communication accommodation. Given that cultural motivation, they can understand strategies of cooperation and participation. Japanese might expect one to sense the context and act in an expected manner, whether the situation calls for proper bowing, silence, or nonverbal expression.

High-context culture is highly dependent on a **hidden culture** — values and rituals are communicated by nonverbal media, and they are hidden in people's potential consciousness. People take them for granted, and there are **tactic understandings** in people's mind. The following table shows the different features of low-high context communication.

Table 3.3 Characteristics of Low-Context and High-Context Communication

Low-Context Communication	High-Context Communication
Linear logic	Spiral logic
Overt and explicit	Covert and implicit
Person-oriented style	Status-oriented style
Self-enhancement style	Self-effacement style
Speaker-oriented style	Listener-oriented style
Verbal-based understanding	Context-based understanding
Details verbalized	Much nonverbal coding
Reactions on the surface	Reactions reserved
Flexible in-groups and out-groups	Distinct in-groups and out-groups
Fragile interpersonal bonds	Strong interpersonal bonds
Time highly organized	Time open and flexible

To sum up, the level of context determines everything about the nature of the communication and is the foundation on which all **subsequent** behavior rests (Hall, 1976). Communication is contextual. The cultural context in which human communication occurs is perhaps the most defining influence on human interaction. For a long time, this theory has always been the landmark that guides intercultural communication study.

3.3 Time

Time is a kind of philosophical issue, which has something to do with the essence of human being's existence. Life on earth evolves in response to the cycles of day and night and the ebb and flow of the tides. As human evolves, a **multiplicity** of internal biological clocks also develops. These biological clocks now regulate most of the physiological functions of our bodies. It is not surprising, therefore, that human concepts of time grow out of natural association with daily, monthly, and annual cycles.

Cultures develop temporal patterns that define the proper time to do certain things such as sleeping, eating, attending a meeting. In America, we hear people saying, "*Time is money*" and "*He who hesitates is lost*." All Chinese know the Confucian proverb "*Look before you leap*."

Human communication occurs in a physical space and perceptual time. Hall (1959) distinguishes between **monochronic** and **polychronic** time patterns. Western culture has **monochronic time** orientation (M-time) and Eastern culture has **polychronic time** orientation (P-time). Time orientation is of vital importance to the intercultural communication research since it acts as a mirror to reflect a culture's deep value structure, life philosophy as well as life style. (Li Mengyu, 2008)

3.3.1 Monochronic Time Orientation

Monochronic time orientation **accentuates** the objectiveness, absoluteness and fixation of time. The concept of the overwhelming power of time is pervasive in the western culture, which is deeply rooted in western civilization. Time has been perceived from the physical aspect. Aristotle in his famous book *Physics* defined time as a measurable object in motion. The scientists and philosophers after the Renaissance followed Aristotle's suit, and they thought of time as a kind of object in linear motion as well. This interpretation of absolute time as the object in motion has been the main time orientation in the western civilization.

In western culture, time is often believed to be something definite, absolute and valuable, which are even used to measure profit and achievement, and there are many famous sayings which express the importance of time: "*The early bird catches the worm*" (the United States), "*Never put off till tomorrow what you can do today*" (England).

In western monochronic culture, time is experienced and used in a linear way — comparable to a road extending from the past into the future. Monochronic time is divided quite naturally into segments; it is scheduled and compartmentalized, making it possible for a person to concentrate on one thing at a time. In a monochronic system, the schedule may take priority above all else and be treated as sacred and unalterable. People perceive time as a linear progression, marching time from the past into the future. They treat time as a tangible, discrete entity, which can be saved, killed, divided and even bought. Cultures like those of the United States and most of Europe tend to use monochronic time patterns.

Monochronic time is perceived as a classification system for ordering life and setting priorities. Because monochronic time concentrates on one thing at a time, people who are governed by it don't like to be interrupted. Monochronic time seals people off from one another and, as a result, intensify some relationships while shortchanging others. Time becomes a room which some people are allowed to enter, while others are excluded.

M-time culture places more emphasis on efficiency and promptness. M-time people concentrate on the job, take time commitment (deadline, schedules) seriously, adhere to plans, being concerned about not disturbing others, and follow rules of privacy.

3.3.2 Polychronic Time Orientation

Polychronic time orientation conceives time to be subjective, relative, and flexible. People in polychronic time cultures tend to treat time in a holistic way. They tend to engage in several activities at the same time. They emphasize the completion or result of transaction rather than adherence to schedules. When they have an appointment or attend a meeting, being late is quite normal. The sense of time or punctuality is slim.

Polychronic time is characterized by the simultaneous occurrence of many things and by a great involvement with people. There are more emphases on completing human transactions than on holding to schedules. For example, two polychronic Arabians conversing on a street corner would be more likely to be late for their next appointment rather than abruptly terminate the conversation before its natural conclusion. Polychronic time is experienced less tangible than monochromic time.

As it is well known, the Chinese culture is greatly influenced by Confucianism. Time orientation in Confucianism is the past-present time focus. Confucius lived in the Spring and Autumn period, a time when wars broke out frequently and there was a decline in social morality. He was very dissatisfied with the situation and intended to reform society by looking back to the past for a good model. His real intention was to express his appreciation for the men in the past and to pass criticisms upon the degeneration of the men in his time. Lastly, Confucianism holds a flexible attitude towards time. It accentuates "the right occasion" and "the right opportunity" in dealing with affairs. Whatever things they might be, whether they are issues concerning big events of the state or trivial household matters, they all should be performed on a right occasion (Li Mengyu, 2008).

Besides being influenced by Confucianism, Chinese time orientation is also influenced by Taoism. Taoism in essence is a philosophy of pursuing the limitless freedom by breaking through various boundaries and restrictions. As far as time dimension is concerned, Taoism advocates the relativity and limitlessness of time, because of the pursuit of freedom and its unique philosophy of relativity towards life.

The **cult** of idle life can also be observed in the ordinary Chinese people's lives at the present time although more and more Chinese people, especially people in the big cities begin to have a quick life pace. Nevertheless, many ordinary Chinese people of older age still prefer to spend some time in chatting with their friends, relatives or neighbors to enjoy the carefree life. Also, it is quite common scene that a working staff is talking in the phone with eyes focusing on the computer screen.

The following table compares the characteristics of monochronic and polychronic time orientation. It reveals how time orientation influences the attitudes of people towards work, the way people socialize and deal with interpersonal relations.

Table 3.4 Monochronic Versus Polychronic Time Orientation

MONOCHRONIC PEOPLE	POLYCHRONIC PEOPLE
do one thing at a time	do many things at a time
concentrate on the job	are highly distractible and subject to interruptions
take time commitments (deadlines, schedules) seriously	consider time commitments an objective to be achieved, if possible
are low-context and need information	are high-context and already have information
are committed to the job	are committed to people and human relationships
adhere religiously to plans	change plans often and easily
are concerned about not disturbing others; follow rules of privacy and consideration	are more concerned with those who are closely related (family, friends, close business associates) than with privacy
show great respect for private property; seldom borrow or lend	borrow and lend things often and easily
emphasize promptness	base promptness on the relationship
are accustomed to short-term relationships	have strong tendency to build lifetime relationships

(*Adapted from Understanding Culture Difference: by Edward T. Hall and Mildred Reed Hall, Intercultural Press, 1987*)

Proper understanding of the differences between the monochromic and polychromic time orientations will be helpful for us to handle business affairs and communicate with people in various cultures.

New Words and Phrases

explicit /ɪkˈsplɪsɪt/ *adj*. 明确的;清楚的
implicit /ɪmˈplɪsɪt/ *adj*. 含蓄的;暗示的
value 价值观
filial piety /ˈfɪlɪəlˈpaɪəti/ 孝顺
individualism 个人主义
collectivism 集体主义
pragmatic /prægˈmætɪk/ *adj*. 实际的;实用主义的
roundabout /ˈraʊndəbaʊt/ *adj*. 迂回的,绕道的
conformist /kənˈfɔːmɪst/ *n*. 墨守成规的人
enshrine /ɪnˈʃraɪn/ *vt*. 被铭记,被奉为神圣
ethos /ˈiːθɒs/ *n*. 民族精神,气质
remunerate /rɪˈmjuːnəreɪt/ *vt*. 酬劳;给予报酬;赔偿
fatalistic /ˈfeɪtəlɪstɪk/ *adj*. 宿命论的
low-key /ˈləʊˈkiː/ *a*. 克制的,低调的
hybridism /ˈhaɪbrɪdɪzəm/ *n*. 杂交,混合性
high-context 高语境
low-context 低语境
cultural continuum 文化意识流
immediacy /ɪˈmiːdɪəsi/ *n*. 直接
manifest culture 显性文化
beat around the bush 旁敲侧击,说话绕圈子
a sound bite 简短讲话
extraneous /ɪkˈstreɪnɪəs/ *adj*. 无关的
in bullet points 以条目列出
hidden culture 隐性文化
tactic understandings 心照不宣
subsequent /ˈsʌbsɪkw(ə)nt/ *adj*. 后来的,随后的
multiplicity /ˌmʌltɪˈplɪsɪti/ *n*. 多样性

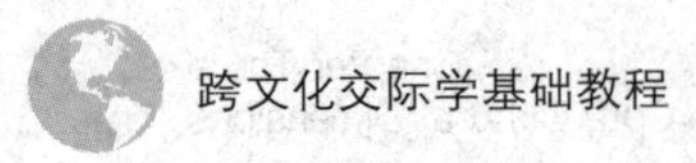

monochronic time 单元时间
polychronic time 多元时间
accentuate /æk'sentjʊeɪt; -tjʊ-/ *vt*. 强调
cult /kʌlt/ *n*. 崇拜,狂热

Exercises

I. Questions for discussion

1. Give examples to demonstrate how values decide one's behaviors.
2. Consider the following two philosophical statements: "I think, therefore I am" and "I am, because we are." What do these two statements reveal about the underlying cultural orientations of those who use them?
3. What are the main characteristics of individualism and collectivism? Do you feel you belong to an individualistic or collectivistic culture? Why?
4. Do you prefer high-context communication or low-context communication? Why?
5. What are the main differences between monochronic time and polychronic time?

II. Multiple choices

Directions: Choose the best answer to each of the following questions.

1. What are the core dimensions in intercultural communication?
   A. value, context and time
   B. beliefs, heroes and rituals
   C. individualism and collectivism
   D. high-context and low-context
2. Which country does not have a typical individualistic orientation?
   A. America　　B. The Netherland
   C. German　　D. China
3. What is the main value harbored in most Chinese people's minds?
   A. Obedience　　B. Filial Piety　　C. Harmony　　D. Respect
4. Which proverb does not indicate individualism?
   A. The squeaky wheel gets the grease.

B. God help those who help themselves.

C. Out of mouth comes evil.

D. Every man is the architect of his own fortune.

5. Which one indicates a typical character of communication in the high-context culture?

A. If you have any suggestion to your leader, tell him without hesitation.

B. You value highly your employee's face when you are supposed to criticize him.

C. I always make details clear when I talk to someone.

D. The whole company works great only because of my personal ability.

III. Comprehension check

Directions: Decide whether the following statements are true (T) or false (F).

1. ________ Cultural context is one of the most important dimensions in intercultural communication.
2. ________ American people are selfish because of their individualistic orientation.
3. ________ Communication style may differ for a teacher and a student when they are in the formal classroom and in a shopping center.
4. ________ Monochronic time orientation is always better than polychronic time orientation in dealing with friend relationships.
5. ________ People in collectivistic society usually think highly of harmony.
6. ________ Time orientation has nothing to do with value orientation.
7. ________ Low-context communication is characterized by explicit speaking.
8. ________ "Time is money" is also popular in China, and that is to say most Chinese have monochromic time orientation.

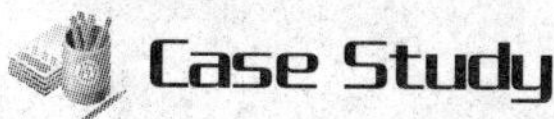

Case I

A female **neurologist**（神经病学家；神经科专门医师）from Beijing was working on a research project in a Toronto hospital. She shared a small office with a young Canadian male from a large family, who loved peanut butter. He was so fond of peanut butter that he kept a jar in the office. One day he came into the office and exclaimed, "Who took my peanut butter?" Chinese woman immediately felt accused. After all, there were only two of them in the office.

She was deeply depressed, but due to her learned cultural behavior of never showing anger in public, she said nothing. Later that day she was working in a room where the Canadian, a **therapist**（理疗师）, was treating a patient who suffered **paralysis**（麻痹；无力）of his legs and arms from a motorcycle accident. The therapist moved one of the patient's legs in a way that caused him pain.

"Ouch!" he cried.

"Oh, I didn't do that," said the Canadian. "It was that doctor over there"and he pointed to the Chinese woman.

"How could she have done it since she's on the other side of the room?" the patient pointed out.

"Ah, She has three hands,"the therapist joked.

At these words the Chinese doctor became even more upset. She was so disturbed that she behaved in a way uncharacteristic of her culture. She waited until the patient had gone, and then said to the therapist, "I'm very upset by what you said." The Canadian was taken aback. "What had I said?" "You said I had three hands," the doctor finally choked. "You think I took the peanut butter."

Questions for Discussion

1. Why didn't the Chinese woman do anything even when she felt deeply depressed?
2. What did the Chinese woman feel when he joked "she has three hands"?
3. What cultural differences does this case reveal?

Case Analysis

Communication failure in this case can be attributed to different contexts they are in. The Canadian speaks in a direct and explicit way that reflects low-context communication. Comparatively, the Chinese woman's reaction indicates her high-context culture.

When the Canadian guy asked who took his peanut butter, he really meant, "Where is my peanut butter? I can't find it." He didn't mean anything interrogative or skeptical. The sentence was not clearly properly encoded to the Chinese woman, and his words seemed to be very offensive to the Chinese woman. Later he made a joke of "three hands", he wasn't serious, and he expected the patient to be amused instead of feeling painful. However, the Chinese woman reached an imaginary third hand and felt totally depressed, because Chinese regard three hands as a nickname for a thief.

Case II

Mr. Paul Bersik is the international sales representative for his computer equipment company. His most recent trip took him to Saudi Arabia, where he was scheduled to meet with his Saudi counterpart, Abdul Arami. Mr. Bersik and his training team arrived in Saudi Arabia three days ago for a schedule appointment with Mr. Arami. Mr. Arami had not yet met with Mr. Bersik or his team. Finally, a call to Mr. Bersik's hotel room indicated that Mr. Arami was prepared to meet with him. When he arrived at the location, Mr. Bersik was asked to wait outside Mr. Arami's office. As he waited, he noticed many people entering and leaving Mr. Arami's office at a very quick pace. The hallways of this building were a hustle and bustle of activity with people shuffling in and out of many rooms. Finally, after several hours, Mr. Bersik was called to meet Mr. Arami.

Mr. Bersik: Ah, Mr. Arami, it's so good to finally see you. Gosh, I've been waiting for days. Did you forget our appointment?

Mr. Arami: Hello Mr. Bersik, please sit down. Everything is fine?

Mr. bersik: Actually no ... (phone rings) ... the problem is ...

Mr. Arami: Excuse me ... (takes the phone call and speaks in Arabic. After several minutes he concludes the phone conversation) Yes, now ... everything is fine?

Mr. Bersik: Well, actually, I've got a small problem. You see the computer equipment you ordered ... (a staff person enters the room and hands Mr.

Arami something to sign).

Mr. Arami: Oh, excuse me (signs the document). Yes, now, everything is fine?

Mr. Bersik: As I was saying . . . all of the computer equipment you ordered is just sitting on a ship in the dock. I need your help in getting it unloaded. I mean it's been there for two weeks!

Mr. Arami: Hmmm. I see . . . This is no problem.

Mr. Bersik: Well, if it sits in the heat much longer it could be damaged. Could I get you to sign a work order to have it unloaded by Friday?

Mr. Arami: There is no need for that. The job will get done, insha Allah.

Mr. Bersik: Well, could we set up some kind of deadline? You see, I have a staff of people here waiting to train your people on the equipment. I need to let them know when it will be ready. How about this Friday? Could we do it then? My people are here now and they're waiting to begin training.

Mr. Arami: There is no great rush. We have lived for many generations without this equipment. We can wait a few more weeks, if necessary. This is not a problem.

(Two men enter the room and begin a conversation with Mr. Arami.)

There is little chance that Mr. Aram will sign any kind of work order for Mr. Bersik.

SOURCE: This case is adapted from Copeland, L. (Producer). (1982). Managing the Overseas Assignment [videorecording]. San Francisco: Copeland Griggs.

Note: Insha Allah — meaning "tomorrow if God wills." It is a favorite expression of the traditional Arab. Arabs believe that time is controlled by Allah. Hence, when trying to schedule an appointment, the Arab may respond "insha Allah".

Questions for Discussion

1. Why does Mr. Arami say "There is no great rush" when Mr. Bersik suggests to set up some kind of deadline?
2. Do the two people have the same time orientation?
3. What cultural differences does this case reveal?

Case Analysis

Communication failure can be attributed to different time orientation in this case. In Saudi culture, people have polychronic time orientation, which means people do many things at one time, and they do not value deadlines. To Mr. Arami, Mr. bersik is too much of a hurry and his behavior is inappropriate. When Mr. Arami says to Mr. Bersik that the job will get done "insha Allah," he means it quite literally. Unless God decrees it, a plan or schedule is useless. Emphasis on deadlines is perceived by Mr. Arami as either insane or irreligious.

In coutrast, Mr. Bersik is also distressed by the constant interruptions. In the future, Mr. Bersik must learn that the Saudis' perception of time is very different from his own. Mr. Bersik is monochromic whereas Mr. Arami is polychromic. When he does business in Saudi Arabi, Mr. Bersik must understand the temporal feature of the culture.

Further Reading

Reading I

Confucius and Confucianism

Confucius (551—479 B. C.), whose given name was Qiu and courtesy name Zhongni, is the founder of Confucianism. Confucious, an intellectual like the Greek philosopher Socrates, is known for his wit and great wisdom. As one of the greatest thinkers and educators in the history of China, Confucius' **legacy** (遗产) lies in the following three aspects. Firstly, he compiled and preserved **literary works** (文学作品) of the generations. Secondly, Confucius established a system of philosophical thoughts with "*Ren*" as its fundamental virtue. Thirdly, Confucius established private schools and founded a systematic educational framework.

Figure 3.3 Confucius

Confucianism is not a religion but a set of practical principles and ethical rules for daily life. Derived from what Confucius understood as the lessons of Chinese history, these ideas have long held a central place not only in China but also in Japan, North and South Korean, and many Asian countries with large Chinese communities.

Confucius is the founder of Confucian school. His **doctrine**（教义、学说）covers various areas, with ritual and *Ren*（human-heartedness and **benevolence**（仁慈；善行））as its central concerns. His followers, who regularly surrounded him and recorded his teachings, provided us with his ideas that we now know of.

Confucius who set up an ethnical-moral system intended ideally to govern all relationships in the family, community, and state. Confucius argued that society was made up of five relationships: those between ruler and subjects (the relation of righteousness), husband and wife (chaste conduct), father and son (love), elder brother and younger brother (order), and between friends (faithfulness). Each of these relationships presumes the existence and legitimacy of a social hierarchy and the **reciprocal**（相互的）, complementary obligations that each position in the hierarchy requires. The higher-status people must provide protection and consideration, while the lower-status people owe respect and obedience.

Three of these five relations occur within the family. The regulation factors in family relationships are extended to the whole community and state. The chief virtue is filial piety, a combination of loyalty and reverence, which demands that the son honor and respect his father and fulfill the demands of his elders.

Confucianism emphasizes virtue, selflessness, duty, **patriotism**（爱国主义）, hard work, and respect for hierarchy, both familial and societal. Teaching and learning are highly valued, moderation in all things is preferred, **conspicuous**（显著的）consumption is frowned, losing one's temper is unacceptable, and persistence in solving difficult problems is widely valued. Because human nature is assumed to be inherently good, it is the responsibility of each individual to train his or her moral character in the behavior standards.

The collectivist values of Confucianism mandate a style of

communication in which respecting the relationship through communication is very important. Group harmony, avoidance of losing face to others and oneself, and a modest presentation of oneself are means of respecting the relationship. One does not say what one actually thinks when it might hurt others in the group.

Confucianism is an important part of the Chinese culture. We should hold a critical attitude to inherit and **assimilate** (吸收；使同化) the fine elements of our national culture. With the development of globalization, it is a realistic and wise alternative to push the Chinese culture into the culture of the world.

Reading II

Time

Time is money

Imagine there is a bank that credits your account each morning with $86,400. It carries over no balance from day to day. Every evening it deletes whatever part of the balance you fail to use during the day. What would you do? Draw out every cent, of course!

Each of us has a bank. Its name is TIME. Every morning, it credits you with 86,400 seconds. Every night it writes off, as lost, whatever of this you have failed to invest in good purpose. It carries over no balance. It allows no **overdraft** (透支). Each day it opens a new account for you. Each night it burns the remains of the day. If you fail to use the day's **deposits** (存款), the lost is yours. There is no going back. There is no drawing against the "tomorrow".

You must live in the present on today's deposits. Invest it so as to get from it the utmost in health, happiness, and success! The dock is running. Make the most of today. And remember that time waits for no one.

Time is rhythm

In Asia, time is more like the rhythm of the waves, the **ebb** (退潮) and flow of hourly, daily, annual and historical cycles. Pay attention to these rhythms and stay in tune with them. Each activity has its time. It is a pleasure to enjoy the strawberries when they come into season. They will only be available for a few weeks, so enjoy them and do not think about them when time is not right.

It is the same with the day. There is a time to work, a time to rest, a time to eat, a time to enjoy friends. Don't worry to impose an unnatural rhythm on the day by skipping meals or working when you should be with your family and friends. If you miss a dear friend today, don't worry. The cycle will come around again, and there will be another right time to meet.

Pay attention to the past. It is a **cushion**（垫子）that softens the pressure of life. It is a **reservoir**（蓄水池）of the wisdom of your ancestors. It is the precious life experience accumulated by your parents and grandparents who lovingly pass it on to you. It is where all our rich humanity, including virtue, can be found in the endless stories of heroes, leaders, scoundrels, enemies, lovers, and sages. Be thankful for them, as they never fail to guide and help you.

The future is where you are going and where you hope to prove yourself worthy of your inheritance from the past. It is where you live out the virtues you have learned and where you pass on your inheritance to those who will come after you, to your children, students, friends, and countrymen. It is where you join your ancestors in the drama of history.

Chapter Four

Physical Environment and Culture

● **Objectives**

- ➢ Understand geographical environment and culture.
- ➢ Understand built environment and culture.
- ➢ Understand city architecture styles and culture.
- ➢ Understand house design and culture.
- ➢ Understand the dimension of privacy.
- ➢ Understand the spatial dimension.

● **导读**

文化不仅是一种社会现象也是历史现象，是社会历史的积淀物。一个民族的文化与该民族所处的客观环境以及由此产生的人类实践活动不可分割。在漫长的民族发展历史和民族文化形成的过程中，物理环境发挥了举足轻重的作用。这里所说的物理环境包括地理、气候、城市建筑、城市设计、房屋布局等方面。同时，民族文化也对人们认识环境、改造环境起着至关重要的作用。

基于本国的地理条件和环境气候，中国发展为以小农经济占主导地位的农业社会，并在此基础上形成了相应的政治制度和意识形态。“天人合一”的哲学思想影响了中国的建筑风格，使中国建筑讲究中轴对称以及与周边环境的和谐。而以希腊文化为起源的西方文化则基于丰富的水域资源，发展为以海洋文化为主导的商业社会。受“天人相分”哲学思想的影响，西方建筑以巨大的体量和超然的尺度来呈现艺术的永恒，富有严密的几何形状，形成傲然屹立，与自然对峙的特点。

Text

4. 1 Geography and Culture

Physical environment includes geography, climate, city architecture/building, city design and room design in a house, spatial dimension, etc. Mountains or flat terrain, barren or fertile land, and the availability of resources would affect human institutions and thereby alter the forms of social behavior. For instance, an abundant water supply or a certain type of soil condition shapes the economy of a region and certainly influences the day-to-day lifestyles of people. The following will take the formation of Chinese culture and western culture as examples of how geographical environment affects culture and communication.

China is a **unitary** multinational country with a vast territory and a large population. The geographical surroundings play a vital role in the formation and development of the Chinese culture. Situated in the East Asia continent, China is located in relatively enclosed geographical surroundings. In the north stretch the vast desert and prairie. In the west lie the vast expanse of Gobi desert and Qinghai-Tibet **plateau**. In the southwest stand Yunnan-Guizhou mountainous region and boundless tropical rain forest. The east and southeast face the ocean.

The relatively enclosed geographical surroundings provide exceptional natural advantages for the ancient Chinese culture to develop independently for a fairly long period free from the impact of foreign cultures, especially those powerful ones. These facilitate the Chinese culture to evolve into a stable and independent system with distinctive regional features.

Since the **terrain** of China is high in the west and low in the east, several long rivers running from west to east are distributed evenly to form the valleys of Liaohe River, Yellow River, Yangtze River and Pearl River. The large rivers and their tributaries facilitate the agricultural development and transportation as well as the growth of regional cultures. Different regional cultures enrich the connotation of Chinese culture. Chinese cultural system is an organic unity with multi-elements, cultural fusion and political unity.

Due to its abundance and variety of natural recourses, the Yellow River Valley, for quite a long time, has been regarded as the major birthplace and base of the ancient Chinese civilization. Especially in the Yellow River Valley and the Yangtze River Valley, farming is the major economic mode. Agricultural civilization plays a decisive role in forming and promoting Chinese culture, which constitutes its fundamental differences from Western culture. The natural geographical location decides the agricultural cultural characters in China; hence group orientation based on family or friend relations has come into being. In the process of agricultural production, the harvest, to a large extent, relies on the soil condition and weather. Thereby people formed the idea of **oneness of man with nature**.

Western cultures originated from ancient Greek culture. 80% of the Greece is covered by highland and mountains, which makes it scarcely possible to plant in the fields. The natural environment was barren so much so that the ancient Greeks had to fight against the odds to make a living. Accordingly, competitive spirit became the primary principle for all the westerners. In the process of competition, advanced technology played a crucial

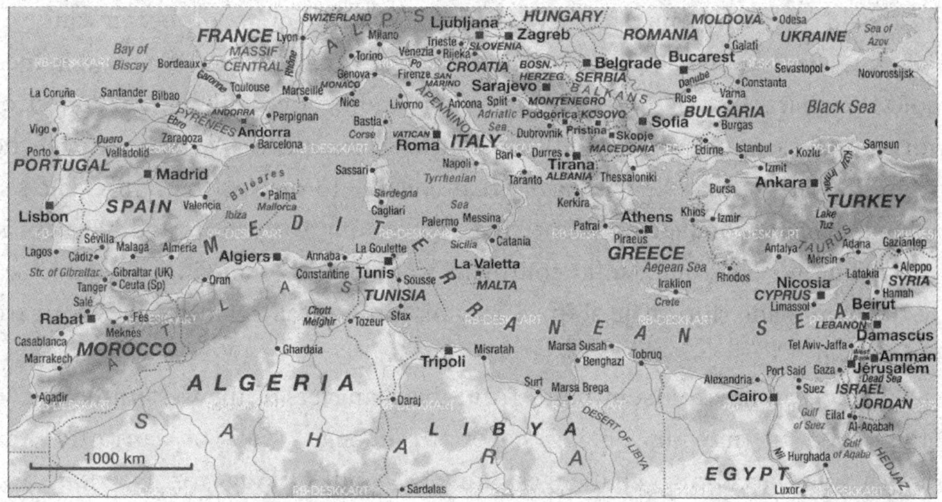

Figure 4.1 Map of Mediterranean Sea

Source: http://www.welt-atlas.de/

role. Consequently, people attach great importance to the science and technology.

The **Mediterranean Sea**, which connects Greeks with each other and with the rest of the world, encompasses the **Aegean Sea**. In the world of the ancient Greeks, the sea were more efficient travel routes because roads were no more than dirty paths. Ships could go much faster and carry much more cargo than wagons bumping over rough terrain. Access to the sea was so critical that most Greek communities were within 60 km of the coast. Places which owned good harbors grew prosperous from the trade that flowed to them and from the fees they could charge ship-owners and merchants.

Ancient Greeks first established a relative democratic, equal contractive society. Eventually, they inhabited about 700 communities clustered around the Mediterranean Sea, which gradually grew into cities. Owing to comparatively small territory of the European countries, the natural resources were limited in each one. Exchanging with others turned into the critical way to get necessities for daily life and raw material for industry. Cities became the place where merchants and businessmen lived. The natural geographical condition decided the commercial cultural characters in the west. Because merchants were always on the move, individual orientation came into being.

Due to the abundant water resources, businessmen's activities occurred mostly on the sea, thus formed the typical characters of ocean culture. Hegel, a well-known German philosopher, explained how the sea helped mold the characters of the western people and establish their perception of world. "The sea offers us boundless, limitless conception. When man feels he is limitless at the sea, he will have great courage to surpass the limit. The sea reminds man of conquering, depriving and seeking for profits and business as well. Man moved from a solid continent to a moving/changing /unstable sea by the man-made ship. The ship, a seagull, sails in sea against waves forward and forward."

The ocean environment helps form the characters of the western people — being good at moving, being eager to change, full of curiosity and competition, accepting challenges bravely, and seeking for freedom and equality.

In addition to the influence on cultural concept, different geographical conditions also help to form different cultural characters. Such differences also can be seen in the diverse metaphors in different languages for the same thing. Let's take China and the UK for example. The former is a typical agricultural society, and the latter is oceanic one. If man drinks heavily, Chinese would say, "He drinks like a cattle"; while Englishman would say, "He drinks like a fish". If one spends a lot of money, Chinese would say, "He spends money like soil" while Englishman would say, "He spends money like water". As UK is an island country, many expressions are related to the ocean. For instance, "He is a cold fish" means he is an indifferent person. "He is all at sea" refers to a man who has no idea of what to do and how to do it. "To keep one's head above water" describes a person who struggles to live. And "to miss the boat" is to miss the opportunity.

Different geographical conditions also give people different associations towards the same thing. "East wind" in China, coming from the oceans in the east, is the symbol of spring and warmth. While it is cold and dry in England as east wind comes from the mainland Europe. And "west wind" in China, coming from the mountainous part, is the symbol of chill and wildness. In Ma Zhiyuan's *Autumn Thought*, "Down a worn path, in the west wind, a lean horse comes plodding" presents a miserable picture. While "west wind" is moist and comfortable in England, it brings everything back into alive. So the English Romantic poet Percy Bysshe Shelley composed the famous poem *Ode to the West Wind*.

In general, the culture of one nation is closely associated with its physical environment. People perceive the physical environment through their culture and the physical environment also influences their cultural orientation, mode of life and communicative behavior.

4.2 Climate and Culture

Climate such as temperature and humidity is closely related to physical environment. And climatic factors have some influences on people's behavior and characters. For instance, the climate in the south of China is warmer and more humid than that in the north of China. To a large extent, the characters of the inhabitants in the south of China are milder and gentler than those of the inhabitants in the north of China. And climatic variations within cultures also affect communicative styles if the territory of a country is large. People in the north of China seem more direct, open and confirming than people in the south in communication.

Different climates form different diets. For example, as a result of the foggy and cloudy weather, *Sichuan* **Cuisine** features spicy and hot food, which helps to get rid of moisture. Guangzhou Cuisine shows a preference to sweet food, which supplements people with essential nutrient to produce energy. For the hot weather makes man sweat a lot and that surely results in lack of sugar. In the northeastern part of China, **stew**ed dish gives people warmth and energy. Different climates form different dressing styles as well. The extremely high temperature makes the Arab to wear white robe to keep heat out. The great difference in temperature allows Scottish men to wear kilt, a specially-made skirt, which could be easily transformed into a cloak to keep warm during the night. Thus it can be seen that human activities do have much to do with the climate and weather conditions.

4.3 Built Environment and Culture

Built environment is an intentionally designed pattern of spatial relationships between objects and objects, objects and people, and people and people. The built environment of any culture consists mainly of adaptations to the **terrestrial** environment, including architecture, housing, lighting, and landscaping. The built environment artificially changes natural patterns of behavior and human communication. It facilitates or restricts human interaction. The following is the comparison between Chinese architecture and western architecture styles, which reveals the relative connection between building and culture.

Figure 4.2 Beijing Quadrangle

Source: http://www.nipic.com/show/4/79/5030517k31c008fa.html

Architectural styles are partly influenced by different ruling **ideologies**. And such ideas can be reflected from the palace complexes to humble farmhouses. Chinese think highly of **hierarchy**. All the architectures follow the principle that the main structure is the **axis**. And the secondary buildings are set as two wings on either side to form the main room and yard. Different classes own their corresponding building style, color and even roof pattern. One can easily tell the other's social and political position via the building. Take the traditional Beijing quadrangle as an example. It has the characteristics of a yard with rooms surrounded by high four walls under the influence of federal, closed family system. Each yard is like a history channel. It stands for traditional culture. The yard symbolizes classes, family positions, and one's position. When walking on the roads under the high walls, people might feel a kind of pressure. The ideology of collectivism is also reflected in the Chinese architecture and thereby the traditional buildings emphasize the width. Many building units gather together to form an integrated building group.

As for Western people, most of them are devotional disciples, so religious buildings are the representation of the highest skills and techniques. The architectures tend to grow in height and depth in order to express men's worship to the gods and their longing for the heaven. Take the **Parthenon** for example. The dimensions of the base are 69.5 meters by 30.9 meters. The **cella** is 29.8 meters long by 19.2 meters wide, with internal **colonnades** in two tiers, structurally necessary to support the roof. On the exterior, the Doric columns measure 1.9 meters wide and are 10.4 meters high. The Parthenon has 46 outer pillars and 23 inner pillars in total. As westerners advocate individualism which cares much about the individual and the personality, the Western buildings tend to be open, spatial and separated, which will

Figure 4.3 Parthenon in Athens

Source: http://en.wikipedia.org/wiki/File: The_Parthenon_in_Athens.jpg

Figure 4.4 Classical Chinese Garden

Source: www.bestvilla.com.cn

appeal to the people without any distraction.

In traditional Chinese architectures, buildings or building complexes usually take up an entire property but encloses open spaces within itself, such as the open courtyard in the north of China and the "sky well" in the south. This structure expresses Chinese character of being conservative. On the contrary, western architectural practices typically involve surrounding a building by an open yard on the property. The yard can be seen and shared by the people around, because they thought it natural for man to be open.

Chinese people believe in the idea of oneness of man with nature. People advocate that men should keep a harmonious relationship with nature, so Chinese traditional architecture seeks the beauty of nature. One could see beautiful view from the building and the building itself is part of the surrounding settings. The harmony also can be seen in balance pursued by all the Chinese through the bilateral **symmetrical** architectural style.

Westerners hold the idea that nature can be conquered by human beings. Such perception makes their buildings high in altitude and space, which may turn out to be more glorious and significant than the surrounding environment. As the terrain is surely complicated, westerners don't put emphasis on the symmetry in buildings, but flexibly designed instead. And **aesthetic** geometry is fully presented in western architectures. **Colosseum** in Rome, **Louvre Museum** in France, and **Washington Monument** in USA are the perfect examples of the western architectural styles.

Amos Rapoport (1969) argues that the interior of any built environment influences and directs the way activities are carried out, how the family is structured, how gender roles are played, what attitudes they hold toward privacy, and what the overall process of social interaction is. Moreover, how the built environment is planned and constructed reflects the values,

Figure 4.5 Colosseum in Rome

Source: http://www.51yougo.com/photos/photo.aspx? id=830

Figure 4.6 Louvre Museum in France

Source: www.uuyoyo.com

motivations, and resources of the culture wherein it exists. The overall economic, political, and legal system of a particular culture affects how that culture designs the built environment, including homes, school, government, and private business buildings. As the built environment of cultures differs, so do communication patterns. Built environment organizes and manages human communication between people, and it varies considerably across cultures.

The different social systems, different cultural **mentalities**, different ruling ideas, or even the different religious thoughts, etc. can be the partial causes of the distinctions in architecture. People shape the built environment according to their cultures. The physical structure of buildings, as well as the way people decorate them is influenced by the cultures in which they exist and also influences the interaction occurring within cultures.

4.4 City design and Culture

Winston Churchill, the former English prime minister, once said, "We construct buildings and buildings mold us as well." In fact, the architectural styles of a city, its physical structure and its internal design styles are influenced by the existing culture while it affects the mode of life, characters and interactive activities of the local people as well.

Oneness of man with nature is the fundamental worldview for the

Chinese. The **layout** of the city also abides by this principle. City planning should be in harmony with the natural beauty. The integration of man-made architectures and the natural landscapes delight the people's eyes and soul. City planning would take the natural environment into consideration. As for the westerners, humanism is their principal belief, which indicates people to be the master of nature. Therefore, European city planning generally follow the rule that artificial buildings are in the urban districts with the natural landscapes in the suburban areas and outskirts. Parks in the downtown are man-made structures to show the capacity of human beings.

Rites of the Zhou, a classical book in Western Zhou Dynasty, puts forward the ideal pattern for the capital city. The center is for the leaders to indicate their supreme power. So the palaces of past dynasties are all on the axis of a city, such as the Luoyang in Northern Wei Dynasty, Chang'an in Tang Dynasty, Beijing in Ming and Tsing Dynasty, etc.

In 500 BC, ancient Greek planner Hippodamus proposed city pattern of the **grid** streets with the square as the center, which revealed their pursuit for freedom. Around the squares and parks were some public buildings for the mass entertainment, such as theatre, stadium, arena, etc. Those were the places where the citizens could assemble for recreation and refreshment. It was based on the democratic idea. Such thoughts are so influential that they still have a far-reaching impact on the respective countries. The design and their architectural projects of the following two cities reveal the styles of eastern and western cultures.

The following two famous cities can best reveal the city designs of eastern and western cultures.

Beijing is the capital and political center of China. Beijing is one of the largest cities in the world. It is a city full of culture. The Great Wall, Summer Palace, Tian An Men Square, palaces, city buildings, temples, narrow streets and old houses all contain culture and have their stories.

The Forbidden City is the Chinese imperial palace from the mid-Ming Dynasty to the end of the Qing Dynasty. It is the largest, best-preserved mass group of halls in China. Located in the center of Beijing, the entire palace area, rectangular in shape and 72 hectares in size, is surrounded by walls ten

Figure 4.7 Forbidden City — the Hall of Supreme Harmony (Taihe Dian)

Source: www.dgju.com

meters high and a **moat** 52 meters wide. At each corner of the wall stands a watchtower with a double-eave roof covered with yellow **glaze** tiles. The red and yellow used on the palace walls and roofs are symbolic. Red represents happiness, good fortune and wealth. Yellow is the color of the earth on the **Loess Plateau**, the original home of the Chinese people. Yellow became an imperial color during the Tang dynasty, when only members of the royal family were allowed to wear it and use it in their architecture. And the Forbidden City locates on the axis of the city of Beijing, indicating their highest unshakable imperial power. In addition, it was specially preserved to serve the royal family and the average man had no access to even taking a look at the inside.

New York is the business and financial center in the United States. It is the largest city in America. There are skyscrapers and prosperous areas such as Empire State Building, Status of Liberty, Financial Market, commercial zones, shuttling cars, hundreds of museums, theatres, street artists, picture shows on streets, various snacks, splendid restaurants, theatres, clubs and bars, etc. The city is arranged in a grid pattern of right-angled streets. The streets running east and west are numbered in sequence. The north-south streets are also numbered in sequence but are called avenues. The orderly arrangement of streets and avenues are good reflections of urban culture of

New Yorkers. And the parks and squares in the city function as the public facilities to provide people places to take a rest and enjoy their leisure time, such as New York's Central Park, Times Square, etc.

The cultural features of the two cities are sharply different. Beijing is a sensitive, cyclic, cultural, traditional, historic city while New York is a rational, linear, practical, modern, future city. The life pace in Beijing is slow and quiet while the life pace in New York is rapid, competitive and risky. People in Beijing interact in a round way while people in New York communicate and interact directly and frankly.

4.5 House Designs and Culture

Figure 4.8 Japanese Folk House

The physical environment influences the way houses are designed and the house design is strongly influenced by cultures. There are great variations in the construction and perception of houses in Japan, German, and America.

In traditional Japanese homes, rooms are separated by *shoji*, meaning sliding screens. A *shoji* is usually made of **cedar lattice** with **translucent** paper stretched over it. *Shoji* is very lightweight and easily slide open or closed with one finger. The purpose and major advantage of *shoji* is that they can be removed easily to convert an entire floor of a house into a single open room. One room in Japanese house has many functions. It can be used for dining, entertaining, and sleeping. Floors in traditional Japanese homes are covered with straw mats, and people remove their shoes when they enter houses. A low table is usually put in the center of the room for many purposes. They may be used for studying and eating. It can be taken away when it is time for sleep. The furniture and decoration in the traditional Japanese homes express the group identity and the communal desire of being together. Doors can be opened by any people in the family. Family members live together to develop the close family relations and create a large family harmonious mood. Japanese house design is beneficial to develop and strengthen group and collectivism orientation.

German homes tend to be surrounded by hedges and fences to ensure privacy. A house is built with particular rooms to fill specific purposes. An ideal German home has an entryway that leads visitors into the house without exposing them to specific rooms. A house is characterized by large furniture and heavy walls. Doors in a house have several functions. One function is that doors are used to serve as a soundproofing so that they can satisfy the desires for privacy. Another function of doors is that they keep the integrity of the room and provides a protective boundary between people. The furniture and doors of homes in Germany illustrate the desire of the occupants to differentiate themselves from others.

American house design is various. A house has a sitting room, bedrooms, washing rooms, kitchen, balcony, etc. Each room has its own function. Americans like to hold parties and invite friends at home. Kitchen, sitting room, bedrooms are places for guests to socialize. When the door of a room is open to guests, it implies guests can enter freely. Once doors are closed, it implies that no one is welcome to enter. In the United States, kitchens have become centers for family members to exchange information because it is a room for family members to gather each day. After taking meals at table, each leaves home to deal with his own affairs. It is very common to see many notices (paper, poster) on the frig door to show some information. For example, "Dad, I am coming home late — I am going to a party with Jane tonight."

In fact, the development of the society push the changes in physical environment that lead to changes in one's mode of living and mode of communication. The environment reflects the openness or closeness of the occupants to outsiders. The differences reflected in the construction of a house and the laying out of furniture are somewhat related to individualism or collectivism.

4.6 Privacy

Irwin Altman (1975) points out that privacy is a selective control of access to self or to one's group. He argues that privacy is a "boundary control" process whereby people sometimes make themselves accessible to others and sometimes close themselves off from others. Privacy is a common phenomenon. It exists in each culture. Although the need for privacy is innate and universal, the degree to which an individual human feels the need for protection varies considerably across cultures.

Americans value privacy so much that they have made it law. Junior high school students learn that Article Four of the Bill of Rights of the Constitution of the United States guarantees every citizen the right to be secure in their persons, houses, papers, and effects against unreasonable searches and seizures. Americans with individual orientation are fond of the word "private". They like to own private car, private room, private telephone, private bathroom, and private doctor. People, who interact with others, walk on the street, or go shopping, have a private zone. They would like to arrange their affairs as their own wills such as time schedules for working, for entertaining, for socializing, etc. All these affairs are private ones. Unscheduled visit to a friend may be rejected as it is taken for the intrusion of personal life. Appointment should usually be made a week ago. Doors are there for knocking, even parents should do so before entering their kid's room. Privacy is protected by laws. In American culture, age, salary, position, religious belief, private letters, family relations, sexual life, friendship, past mistakes or crimes, diseases, hobbies, healthy conditions, family background, and possessions are all regarded as privacy. The American poet Robert Frost once said, "Good fences make good neighbors." Each person minds his own business and any interference would be regarded as offensive.

Chinese are inclined to lay emphasis on people in their group in order to maintain a kind of group harmony. Hence the above private matters are socially concerned in China. Chinese people often ask their friends or other people the questions about their personal life, such as income, marriage, belief. People often ask questions such as "Have you had your supper/meal/lunch/breakfast?" "How old are you?" "Are you married?" "May I introduce a boyfriend to you?" "How much do you earn each month?" "Where are you going?" "How much money do you spend in buying your house?" These questions are acceptable in China. They make the listeners feel warm, close, and safe. In China, people may pay a visit to others without an appointment. However, the above questions will be regarded as a behavior to intrude privacy in America.

In all, privacy is a necessary condition for acceptable social behavior. Knowing a culture's preferences about privacy can help us know when and how a culture desires privacy, we would know when to restrict communication with people from that culture.

4.7 Spatial Dimension

Different cultures adopt different measures to control their own field. Some cultures protect privacy by means of physical environment. Others protect privacy by means of psychological control.

Figure 4.9 Great Wall in China
www.nipic.com

In China, walls and fences are built to protect family or group space and interests. People are separated by fences or walls. Chinese culture is famous for its walls: from the Great Wall to Summer Palace; from walls of villages to walls of yards; from brick walls to fences in the fields. Walls exist everywhere in cities and the countryside in China. Nearly all houses, factories, parks, schools, office buildings are surrounded by walls. There are high, low, narrow, or broad walls, made of earth, brick, steel, wood, or bamboo, etc. Walls in China symbolize the conservative mind of people. In communities, walls or fences hinder people to socialize with their neighbors. Walls are used to protect family, group or business privacy in China.

The Westerners whose culture stresses individualism are used to protecting their own group or family interests with space. They generally demand more space than people from collective cultures do and tend to take an active, aggressive manner when their space is violated. In western cultures, personal territory is highly valued. Each person has his own space at home or in offices that should not be invaded. In public places, they have "temporary territory" which should not be intruded either. For example, if in a park you want to sit on a bench which another person has occupied, you have to ask his permission before sitting down. This shows that you recognize his "temporary territory."

Americans are sensitive to space. They take advantage of space to adjust individual, family, group privacy. Schools, hospitals, factories, houses in American cities are separated by space. It is hard for you to find out or recognize the boundary of a university from its neighbor areas. There is no wall or fence to separate a university from the local areas. There are no walls to separate houses. There is no visible boundary but it does exist. The boundary exists in people's mind. People are clearly aware of the limitation. They would not intrude others' territories or lands without permission. The open space is beneficial for people to socialize with each other.

New Words and Phrases

unitary /ˈjuːnɪtəri/ *n*. 单一的，一元的
plateau /ˈplætəʊ/ *n*. 高原
terrain /ˈtereɪn/ *n*. 地域，地带
Oneness of man with nature 天人合一
Mediterranean Sea 地中海
Aegean Sea 爱琴海
cuisine /kwɪˈzɪn/ *n*. 菜肴
stew /stjuː/ *v*. 炖，煮
terrestrial /tɪˈrestrɪəl/ *adj*. 地球的，陆地的
ideology /ˌaɪdɪˈɒlədʒi/ *n*. 思想体系，思想意识
hierarchy /ˈhaɪərɑːki/ *n*. 等级制度
axis /ˈæksɪs/ *n*. 中轴，轴线
Parthenon 帕台农神殿
cella /ˈselə/ *n*.（古希腊或罗马庙宇之）内殿，内堂
colonnade /ˈkɒləˈneɪd/ *n*. 列柱，柱廊

symmetrical /sɪˈmetrɪkəl/ *adj*. 对称的
aesthetic /iːsˈθetɪk/ *a*. 审美的，美学的
Colosseum 古罗马角斗场
Louvre Museum（法国）卢浮宫
Washington Monument（美国）华盛顿纪念碑
mentality /menˈtælɪti/ *n*. 心态
layout /ˈleɪaʊt/ *n*. 安排，布局
Rites of the Zhou《周礼》
grid /grɪd/ *n*. 格子
moat /məʊt/ *n*. 护城河
glaze /gleɪz/ *n*. 釉
Loess Plateau 黄土高原
cedar /ˈsiːdə/ *n*. 雪松，雪松木材
lattice /ˈlætɪs/ *n*. 格子，格状物
translucent /trænsˈluːsənt/ *adj*. 半透明的

Exercises

I. Questions for discussion

1. Explain with examples that physical environment has an influence on culture.
2. The walls and roofs of Forbidden City employ the color of red and yellow. What are the cultural connotations?
3. What are the characteristics and cultural implications of Gothic architectures?
4. Give a brief contrast of the privacy in the East and West.
5. What way do Chinese and Westerners respectively employ in field protection?

II. Multiple choice

Directions: *Choose the best answer to each of the following questions*.

1. Chinese cultural system is an organic unity. Which of the following element does not contribute to the formation of Chinese culture?

   A. The relatively enclosed geography

B. Agricultural economy

C. Frequent exchanges

D. Group orientation

2. Western culture originated from ________.

A. ancient Babylon (古巴比伦) B. ancient Rome

C. ancient Egypt D. ancient Greece

3. Physical environment has a great impact on the various cultural factors. Such impact can be shown in ________.

A. diet B. dress

C. language D. all of above

4. Cultural orientations of one nation can also be reflected in their architectures. Chinese buildings are generally ________ ones.

A. multi-storied B. symmetrical

C. rocky D. various-shaped

5. Cultural orientations of one nation also can be reflected in their architectures. Western buildings are generally ________ ones.

A. aesthetic geometrical B. wooden

C. cyclic D. low

III. Comprehension check

Directions: *Decide whether the following statements are true* (*T*) *or false* (*F*)

________ 1. Englishmen employ the expression "to drink like a cattle" to describe the person who drinks a lot.

________ 2. West wind is the symbol of strength and warmth because UK is close to the Atlantic Ocean. The famous poem *Ode to the West Wind* is the perfect embodiment.

________ 3. Climatic factors have some influence on people's behavior and characters.

________ 4. Westerners think highly of their privacy while Chinese people have no privacy.

________ 5. Diverse ruling ideologies mold different architectural styles. Hence, imperial palaces are the representation of the highest techniques in China and the counterpart of Western countries are religious buildings.

________ 6. The layout of the city also abides by the cultural orientations.

________ 7. The Westerners whose culture stresses individualism pay much attention to protect their own interests. Therefore, colleges and companies would set up high walls and hedges to safeguard their own field.

________ 8. Since Yellow River, Yangtze River and Pearl River have been the major birthplaces of ancient Chinese civilization, fishing turns out to be the major economic mode.

Case I

Liu Xiaoyan is a Chinese student, who goes to the USA for further education. After living there for a period of time, she observes that Americans like to comment on each other's looks and clothes. In order to make more new friends and become more intimate with other friends, she decides to do so at a party. So at the sight of a fellow graduate student Mary wearing a nice dress, she begins to compliment her.

Liu: Hi, Mary, how are you doing?

Mary: Pretty good. Thank you. How are you doing?

Liu: I'm fine. Oh, your dress is extraordinarily attractive!

Mary: Oh, thank you. (She is very pleased and smiles.)

Liu: Where did you buy it?

Mary: I bought it last week in the Fancy Mall.

Liu: What size do you wear? It may be a little tight for me. Is there a larger one?

Mary: Well, I'm not sure about it. (She looks like a little embarrassed.) You can go to check it.

Liu: How much is it? Is it expensive?

Mary: Well I don't quite remember the price. (She seems unprepared for the question, and answers a little hesitatingly. She looks at the other side.) See, Kate is over there. I haven't seen her for a long time. There're really some important things to discuss with her. I'll catch you later.

Liu: Ok, see you later.

Questions for Discussion

1. Why does Liu want to compliment Mary?
2. Why doesn't Mary want to continue their conversation? What question makes her feel uncomfortable?
3. Given you were Liu, what can help you to get a better relationship with the Americans?

Case Analysis

Americans think seriously of their own privacy. Any interference or inquiry can be taken for the intrusion of personal affairs. Age, salary, position, religious belief, private letters, family relations, sexual life, friendship, past mistakes or crimes, diseases, hobbies, healthy conditions, family background, and possessions are all regarded as privacy.

Liu's compliment on Mary's dress is acceptable and even welcome because westerners have much confidence in themselves and are happy to admit their individual advantages and achievements. Therefore, Mary felt pleased talking with Liu. And their relationship may get closer than before. But the inquiry of money or price is definitely social no-no. Such inquiry would definitely be regarded as mere intrusion of one's privacy, which surely cause embarrassment and aversion in communication. While in China, it is acceptable to talk about the price of items. The more private things you know, the more intimate relationship you have. Hence Liu should make clear of the range of privacy for Americans and show due respect to it.

Case II

Wang Xia is a Chinese, who teaches English in the middle school. During the summer vacation, she gets the opportunity to go to University of California for a two-month summer program. Diana, a professor of University of California, is her tutor. One day, Diana invites Wang Xia to her home for the afternoon tea. While they are having coffee, Diana shows Wang a few pictures of her boyfriend in a photo album.

Diana: Look, this is my boyfriend, Jack.

Wang: Oh, he's so cute.

Diana: Thank you.

Wang: Where did he take this picture? It's a really beautiful garden.

Diana: He was working in Rome last year. That was his backyard. I love it as well. Sitting on the wooden chair and sipping a cup of cappuccino would be the best way to refresh ourselves.

Wang: That's excellent refreshment!

(At that time, Wang casually turns to next page to see other photos. Becoming a little angry, Diana reaches out her arm and presses Wang's hand firmly and quickly.)

Diana: I'd rather you not look at other pictures.

Wang: What's up? I thought you were showing me the whole album.

Diana: This is a family album. Those photos are indeed private. I just want you to see my boyfriend not my family.

Wang: Sorry.

Diana: Ok. Let's put it aside and discuss about the experiment report.

Wang: All right. (But indeed, Wang is very angry and decides to break down their friendship.)

Questions for Discussion

1. What does Wang do to make Diana somewhat angry?
2. Why doesn't Diana allow Wang to see other photos in the album?
3. How can Wang avoid such embarrassments in the future?

Case Analysis

Sharing the pictures and memories is quite natural and common thing among friends and relatives in China. This could make other people know more about their friends and definitely would make their relationship more intimate than before. Pictures are not so private, especially those in an album shown to another person. Many Chinese get to know their friends' family and daily life via seeing their pictures. Diana shows some pictures in her album to Wang, which would be assumed that the whole album could be seen.

Yet as for Americans, privacy is so precious that they have made it law. The Constitution of the United States guarantees every citizen the right to be secure in their persons, houses, papers, and effects against unreasonable searches and seizures. At home, each has his own private room. Even Mom should knock at the door before entering her child's room. In the office, one has his own table. You can't even read your colleague's newspaper on his table because it is privately owned. In this case, the photo album is privately owned by Diana, who has unshakable control over it. Under this circumstance, Wang may ask "Oh these pictures are lovely. May I look at the rest?" to avoid such embarrassment. Only when Wang gets the permission from the owner can she see all the pictures in it. Otherwise, it would be taken as sheer peeking at other's private life, a totally rough and rude behavior.

Further Reading

Reading I

Introduction to Ancient Chinese Architectural Styles

The history of Chinese architecture is as old as that of Chinese civilization. Various evidences strongly prove the fact that the Chinese have always employed an inherent system of construction that has maintained its primary characteristics from prehistoric times to the present day.

Characteristics of Ancient Architectural Styles

Chinese architectures put much emphasis on the balance and symmetry. Royal buildings, folk residences, temples and so forth all follow this principle that the main structure is the axis. The secondary structures are positioned as two wings on either side to form the main room and yard. Bilateral symmetries are found everywhere in Chinese architecture, from palace complexes to humble farmhouses. Such type of construction perfectly reflects the deeply-rooted belief among the Chinese people that human beings should be in harmony with the nature and other people.

Another significant feature of ancient Chinese architectures is the use of timber framework. The wood materials are easily available and the construction approaches are relatively simple, hence they are taken as the first choice for construction. In addition, the springy wooden framework is quake-resistant with the structure of **tenon-and-mortise joints** (榫卯). But wooden materials also hold some disadvantages. For one thing, it is vulnerable to fire. For another, the durability of such buildings is comparatively shorter than those made of stone or rock.

Classification by Structure

Chinese classifications for architecture include:

- Chinese pavilions (亭)
- Terraces (台)
- Multistory buildings (楼)
- Two-story pavilions (阁)
- Verandas with windows (轩)
- Chinese pagodas (塔)
- Pavilions or houses on terraces (榭)
- Rooms along roofed corridors (屋)
- Caisson domed or coffered ceiling (藻井)
- Interlocking wooden brackets(斗拱), often used in clusters to support roofs and add ornamentation

Imperial Architectures

As the critical ingredient of the Chinese glorious culture, the imperial architecture records the great intelligence and creation of the laborious ancient people that had a profound impact on the design of modern architecture at home and abroad. It is the perfect embodiment of the Chinese ancient architecture. The imperial palace shows us their living surroundings. Even after their death, the imperial **mausoleum** is also the integration of arts and crafts.

The Chinese feudal society saw the construction of numerous palaces, built to satisfy the emperors' extravagant lifestyles and protect the dignity of their authority. Served as the venue where public affairs were dealt with and where the royal family lived, the construction of imperial palaces emphasizes the splendid appearance and regular layout. From the E'pang Palace of the

Qin Dynasty (221BC－206BC), Weiyang Palace of the Han Dynasty (206BC－220) to the Forbidden City of the Qing Dynasty (1644－1911), the scale of Chinese imperial palaces became larger and larger. Most of them are axial symmetrical, with splendid buildings standing at the middle axis and smaller attached houses located along both sides.

The Chinese dragon, an **emblem** (象征) reserved for Imperial China, is heavily used on Imperial architecture, especially on the Imperial Palaces — on the roofs, on the beams and pillars, and on the doors. Dragon and phoenix, called Long and Feng in Chinese respectively, are totems (图腾) of Chinese people. They are used to represent emperors and their consorts and are the main decorative patterns to be seen on various imperial structures.

Imperial Mausoleums

Imperial **Mausoleums** (陵墓), presenting the highest architectural techniques of the particular period, reveal the imposing significant manner of royalty. In order to continue their extravagant life after death, the emperors would often force countless architects, spend massive capital and take several decades to accomplish such constructions.

Imperial mausoleums were usually built against hills or mountains and facing plains. The broad ways, named the Sacred Way, locate at the entrance. Along both sides, there are stone sculptures of men and animals which guard the tombs. Under huge hills of clay, splendid and superior structures were constructed with fine facilities such as drainage systems.

Imperial Mausoleums are often called underground palaces. As time goes by, the features are various in different dynasties. The Mausoleum of the First Emperor Qin Shihuang in Xi'an is the perfect embodiment of the emphasis on large scales during the Qin and Han Dynasty. The **Terracotta Army** (兵马俑) attracts thousands of millions of visitors from home and abroad. And being the largest tomb complex in China, the Eastern Qing Tombs also reflect the belief of the harmonious unity of mausoleum construction with nature.

Elegant Garden Architectures

The principle of Chinese gardening is to provide beautiful settings by designing all the elements in a harmonious way. Within them, you can see the mountain, water, building, road, indoor decoration and so forth. The Chinese gardens can be classified into two categories: imperial garden in Beijing and private garden in the south. Each has developed its own distinctive characteristics over the years.

The imperial gardens are famous for expensive size, magnificence and stateliness. The Summer Palace is a monument to classical Chinese architecture, in terms of both garden design and construction. In December 1998, UNESCO included the Summer Palace in its World Heritage List with the following comments:

(1) The Summer Palace in Beijing is an outstanding expression of the creative art of Chinese landscape garden design, incorporating the works of humankind and nature as a harmonious whole;

(2) The Summer Palace epitomizes the philosophy and practice of Chinese garden design, which plays a key role in the development of this cultural form throughout the east;

(3) The imperial Chinese garden, illustrated by the Summer Palace, is a potent symbol of one of the major world civilizations.

In contrast the private gardens take on a different look. The gardens of Suzhou are epitome of landscaping art for the private garden, with their delicacy, intimacy, and simplicity. The designers of private gardens, not bound by the rigid conventions of the imperial court, had greater freedom of expression in their art.

The gardens of Suzhou are usually small ones with artificial hills, trees decorated with natural Chinese scenery and poetry of the Tang and Song Dynasties. The layouts of the pavilions, ponds and bridges build complete and harmonious scenery despite their small size, which could effectively relax and refresh the people inside.

Adapted from *An Outline of Chinese Culture*, Peking University Press, *Professional English in Urban Planning and Architecture*, Tianjin University Press and http://www.ebeijing.gov.cn/Tour/ScenicSpots/

Reading II

Introduction to Ancient Western Architectures

In the long history of the western world, the style of western architectures has varied from country to country. The following is the brief introduction to those typical categories.

The Architecture of Ancient Greece

Architecture was extinct in Greece from the end of the Mycenaean period (about 1200 BC) to the 7th century BC, when native life and prosperity recovered to a point where public buildings could be undertaken.

The temple was the most common and best-known from Greek public architecture. The temple did not serve the same function as a modern church, since the **altar** (圣坛,祭坛) stood under the open sky, often directly before the temple. Other architectural forms used by the Greeks were the circular temple. Inside, the porch formed the entrance to temple; the fountain house was the building where women filled their vases with water from a public fountain; and the **stoa** (拱廊,柱廊) referred to a long narrow hall with an open colonnade on one side, which was used to house rows of shops in the commercial centers of Greek town. Greek towns also needed at least one council **chamber** (会议厅,会场), a large public building which served as a court house and as a meeting place for the town council. Because the Greeks did not use arches or **domes** (圆屋顶,穹窿), they could not construct buildings with large interior spaces. The council chamber thus had rows of internal columns to hold the roof up.

There were two main styles of early Greek architecture, the **Doric order** (多立克柱式) and the **Ionic order** (爱奥尼柱式). The former was more formal and plain, and the latter was more relaxed and decorative. These names were used by Greeks themselves, and reflected their belief that the styles descended from the Dorian and Ionian Greeks of the Dark Ages, but this is unlikely to be true. The Doric style was used in mainland Greece and spread from there to the Greek colonies in Italy. The Ionic style was used in the cities of Ionia (now the west coast of Turkey) and some of the Aegean islands. Most surviving Greek buildings, such as the Parthenon and the Temple of Hephaestus in Athens, are Doric. The **Erechtheum**（伊瑞克提翁庙）and the **Temple of Athena Nike**（雅典娜胜利女神庙）on the **Acropolis**（卫城）are Ionic.

The Architecture of Ancient Rome

The architecture of ancient Rome adopted the external Greek architecture for their own purposes, which were so different from Greek buildings as to create a new architectural style. The two styles are often considered one body of classical architecture. This approach is considered reproductive, and sometimes it hinders scholars' understanding and ability to judge Roman buildings by Greek standards, particular when relying solely on external appearances.

Social elements such as wealth and high population densities in cities forced the ancient Romans to discover new architectural solutions of their own. The use of vaults and arches together with a sound knowledge of building materials, for example, enabled them to achieve extraordinary success in the construction of imposing structures for public use.

Improvements in the use of concrete facilitated the building of the many aqueducts throughout the empire. Ancient Roman concrete was a mixture of **lime mortar**（石灰砂浆）, sand, water, and stones, and stronger than previously-used concrete. The ancient builders placed these ingredients in wooden frames where it hardened and bonded to a facing of stones or bricks. When the framework was removed, the new wall was very strong with a rough surface of bricks or stones.

The Colosseum in Rome is one of the greatest works of Roman architecture and Roman engineering. Capable of seating 50,000 spectators, it was used for **gladiatorial**（斗剑的）contests and public spectacles. Unlike earlier Greek theatres that were built into hillsides, the Colosseum was an entirely free-standing structure.

A triumphal arch is a structure in the shape of monumental archway, in theory built to celebrate a victory in war, actually used to celebrate a ruler. Roman classical triumphal arch was a free-standing structure, quite separate from city gates or walls, but the form is often used in engaged arches as well.

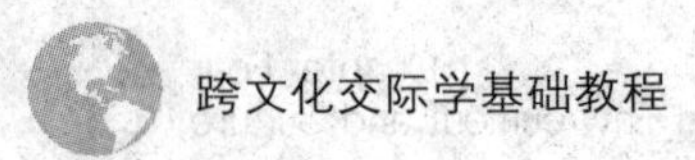

The most famous embodiment may be the Triumphal Arch in Paris.

Gothic Architecture

Gothic architecture is a style of architecture which flourished during the high and late medieval period. It evolved from Romanesque architecture and was succeeded by Renaissance architecture. Originating in 12th century France and lasting into the 16th century, Gothic architecture features in the pointed arch, the ribbed vault and the flying buttress.

Gothic architecture is most familiar as the architecture of many of the great cathedrals, abbeys and parish churches of Europe. It is also the architecture of many castles, palaces, town halls, universities, and to a less prominent extent, private dwellings.

It is in the great churches and cathedrals and in a number of civic buildings that the Gothic style was expressed most powerfully, its characteristics lending themselves to appeal to the emotions. A great number of **ecclesiastical**（教会的，教士的）buildings remain from this period, of which even the smallest are often structures of architectural distinction while many of the larger churches are considered priceless works of art and listed with UNESCO as World Heritage Sites. For this reason a study of Gothic architecture is largely a study of cathedrals and churches.

In Gothic architecture, a unique combination of existing technologies established the emergence of a new building style. Those technologies were the pointed arch, the ribbed vault, and the flying buttress. The Gothic style, when applied to an ecclesiastical building, emphasizes **verticality**（垂直型）and light. This appearance was achieved by the development of certain architectural features, which together provided an engineering solution.

One of the defining features of Gothic architecture is the pointed arch. The structural advantage is that the pointed arch channels the weight onto the bearing piers or columns at a steep angle. This enabled architects to raise vaults much higher. In addition, the use of the pointed arch gave a greater flexibility to architectural form. What's more, it gave the building a very different visual character, the verticality suggesting the longing for Heaven.

Based on the above introduction, the conclusion may be drawn that the styles of western architectures surely are abundant. We should learn to distinguish them.

Adapted from *Professional English in Urban Planning and Architecture*, Tianjin University Press

Chapter Five

Communication and Culture

● **Objectives**

- ➢ Understand the nature of communication.
- ➢ Know the components of communication.
- ➢ Understand the features and styles of communication.
- ➢ Understand communication apprehension & barriers to communication.
- ➢ Acquire some skills for effective communication.
- ➢ Understand the relationship between culture and communication

● **导读**

交际是流动的文化，而文化是冻结了的人际交流。交际是人们通过语言、行为等表达方式交流意见、情感、信息的过程。交际模式由十大要素构成。交际特征主要包括五个方面：符号性、可解读性、相互作用性、语境相关性和动态性。

为实现有效交际，必须弄清影响交际的五大障碍：语言障碍、文化障碍、个人障碍、人际障碍和渠道障碍。文化在很大程度上影响着人们的交际风格，直接型和间接型为两大主要交际风格。交际过程中，了解对方的交际风格和掌握一定的交际技能是进行有效交际必不可少的条件。

Text

5.1 Nature of Communication

According to Longman dictionary, communication refers to the process by which people exchange information or express their thoughts and feelings. Communication is a form of human behavior derived from a need to connect and interact with other human beings. Therefore, communication can simply refer to the act and process of sending and receiving messages among people.

Communication is related to both "communion" and "community". It comes from the Latin "communicare", which means, "to make common" or "to share." The formal study of communication can be traced back to Aristotle's *Rhetoric* 2,000 years ago. Early views of human communication tended to embrace a mechanistic perspective of the communication process. This perspective regards communication as a unidirectional process in which the receivers are passively influenced by powerful sources. Recently, scholars have treated communication as a process in which behaviors can be explained by referring to our intentions, reasons, and goals. It means that interactants are active agents, possessing the ability to choose actions in the interactional process rather than being driven by external factors that determine their behaviors.

Humans employ communication in every aspect of daily life. It serves to facilitate human socialization, maintain social relationships, and develop personality. All communication events, including intercultural ones, are made up of a set of basic features. Concerning the basic ones, communication is a symbolic, interpretive, transactional, contextual, and dynamic process in which people create the shared meaning. Once these features are known, they can be applied to intercultural interactions in order to analyze the unique ways in which intercultural communication differs from other forms of communication.

There are different ways of classifying communication. According to the message, communication may be verbal or non-verbal. Concerning the degree of feedback, communication may be one-way or interactive. In terms of the channel used, communication may be direct or indirect. Viewed from the level of context, communication may be interpersonal, interorganizational and media-based. By means of the cultural background of the sender and receiver, communication may be intracultural and intercultural. In addition, communication may be intrapersonal (communicating with oneself) and interpersonal (communicating with others), intentional and unintentional, successful and unsuccessful communication, effective and ineffective communication, or appropriate and inappropriate communication. Ideally, successful communication should be both effective and appropriate.

5.2 Components of Communication

Within the framework of intentional communication, there are ten components: context, source, message, receiver, channel, noise, response, feedback, **encoding** and **decoding**. Each of them plays an important role in the process of communication and is worth our attention.

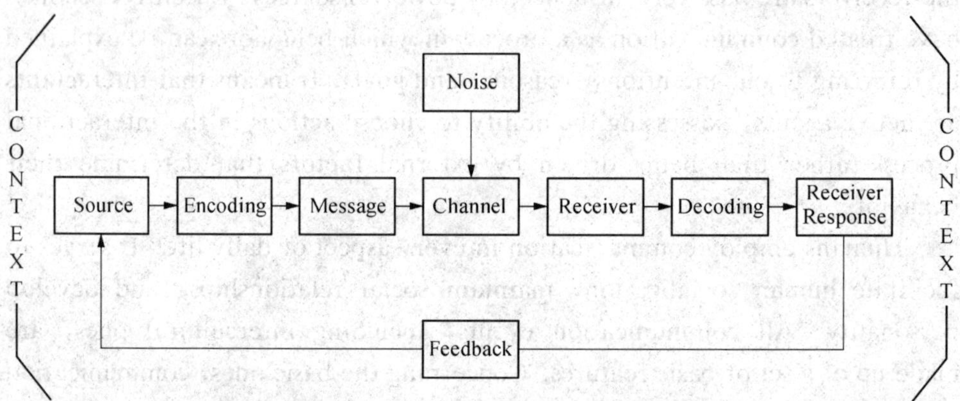

Figure 5.1 Ten Components of Communication

As is shown in the above model, there are ten major components of communication. A *source* is the individual who originates a message by encoding an idea into a message. *Encoding* refers to the process of the sender putting the message into a signal (the encoded message); *Message* identifies the encoded thought. Encoding is the process, the verb; the message is the resulting object. A *channel* is the means by which a message is transmitted from its origin to its destination. *Noise* is anything that interferes with the communication process among participants. A *receiver* is the individual who decodes a communication message by converting it into an idea. *Decoding* refers to the process of the receiver interpreting the signal from the sender. *Receiver response* refers to anything the receiver does after decoding the message. That response can range from doing nothing to taking some actions that may or may not be the action desired by the source. *Feedback* is a message about the effects of a previous message that is sent back to the source. *Context* is the environment in which the communication takes place.

Among the ten **ingredients**, encoding and decoding are of special significance because communication is achieved by encoding a message into a signal and by decoding this signal at the receiving end. Encoding is a process to encode one's ideas, emotions and conceptions into language codes, verbal and nonverbal behaviors and written symbols while decoding is a process to interpret the meaning of information or message and symbols to the outside world. The effective communication builds on the common language codes system shared by the receiver and sender of the messages.

The following is a conversation between two colleagues who meet at the bus station after work. It serves as a useful example to illustrate these ten components. Table 5.1 presents the analysis of the example according to the communication model outlined in Figure 5.1.

A Brief Conversation between Two Colleagues

Tom: Hi, how've you been today?

Mary: Not bad. And you?

Tom: Oh, can't complain. Busy.

Mary: Yeah, me too.

Tom: (The bus Tom will take is coming) Oh well, gotta going home first. See ya.

Mary: Bye. Take care.

Table 5.1 The Ten Communication Components of the Sample Conversation

Components	Explanation of the Components	Illustrations in this conversation
Context	A setting or situation in which communication occurs	The bus station
Sender	The individual who originates a message	Tom
Encoding	The process by which an idea is converted into a message	Converting the idea of greeting into a verbal message
Message	The information being sent	A verbal greeting (How've you been?)
Channel	The means by which a message is transmitted from its origin to its destination	Face-to-face
Receiver	The intended destination of the message	Mary
Decoding	The process by which the message is converted by an idea	Converting the verbal message into the idea of greeting: He's greeting me.
Response	The reaction of the receiver to the decoded message	Positive response to the greeting
Feedback	A message about the effects of a previous message that is sent back to the source	A verbal message sent back: "Not bad. And you?
Noise	Anything that interferes with the transmission of a message	The coming of the bus

One thing worthy of notice is that in this conversation the communication is relatively going on smoothly until the coming of the bus which interferes with the talk. Therefore, the coming of the bus is considered as "noise" of the interaction. Probably, there are some other physical noises while they are waiting for the bus at the station and, thus, the two communicators sometimes may not hear each other perfectly well. However, human communication is never as perfectly effective as this example suggests. The receiver does not always decode a message into exactly the same meaning that the source had in mind when encoding the message. Misunderstandings or even conflicts are especially likely to occur when the source and the receiver lack a common value-base, culture or perspective.

5.3 Features of Communication

All communication events are made up of a set of basic features. Concerning the basic ones, communication is a symbolic, interpretive, transactional, contextual, and dynamic process in which people create the shared meaning.

5.3.1 Symbolic

Symbols are essential to the communication process because they represent the shared meanings that are communicated. A *symbol* is a word, action, or object that stands for or represents a unit of meaning. Meaning, in turn, is a perception, thought, or feeling that a person experiences and might want to communicate to others. People's behaviors are frequently interpreted symbolically, as an external representation of feelings, emotions, and internal states. To many people around the world, for example, thumb-up symbolizes very good or ok. Flags can symbolize a country. To many people in the United States, raising an arm with the hand extended and moving the hand and arm up and down symbolizes saying good-bye. And most of the world's religions have symbols that are associated with their beliefs.

Some symbol systems, such as verbal languages and a special class of nonverbal symbols are completely unrelated to their referents except by common agreement among a group of people to refer to things in a particular way. For instance, a peace symbol is a nonverbal **emblem** that can be displayed by extending the index and middle fingers upward from a clenched fist. The same symbol was used by Winston Churchill to indicate victory, but to many people in South American countries it is regarded as an **obscene** gesture.

However, for many symbol systems, such as most nonverbal and visual ones, the relationship between the symbols and their referents is much less **arbitrary** than that between verbal languages and their referents. Such symbols as a growling stomach when hungry, a child's tears when sad, or a portrait that details a person's facial features are all so **intrinsically** associated with their referents that the range of expected meanings is very restricted. However, these types of symbols are useful precisely because much less knowledge of a specific language and culture is required to understand them. Thus, international traffic symbols, which consist of easily understood pictures, are frequently used in place of words to instruct drivers. Competent intercultural communicators must learn to "read" the symbols to understand the implication and get the exact meanings.

5.3.2 Interpretive

Communication is always an interpretive process. Whenever people communicate, they must interpret the symbolic behaviors of others and assign significance to some of those behaviors in order to create a meaningful account of the others' actions. But during the actual **episodes** involving intercultural communication, people interpret the meanings of messages differently.

Many people incorrectly use the word communication to represent an acceptable level of similarity or agreement in their conversations. They might use the phrase "I really could communicate with her" when they have had a very pleasant conversation in which the other person expressed a similar point of view, or they might say "I just can't communicate with him any more" when disagreements exist. These errors confuse two very different outcomes of the communication process.

The first outcome of communication is that the participants understand what the others are trying to communicate. Understanding means that the participants have imposed similar or shared interpretations on what the messages actually mean. Indeed, without some degree of understanding between the participants, it would be inaccurate to claim that communication has even occurred. Thus, failed attempts at communication, such as when an accident victim calls for help and no one is nearby to hear, are not actually communication.

The second outcome is reaching *agreement* on the particular issues that have been discussed. Agreement means that each participant not only understands the other's interpretations but also holds a similar view. However, although understanding is a necessary ingredient to say that communication has occurred, agreement is not a requirement of communication. It is possible, and often quite likely, that people will understand one another's position or ideas yet not agree with them.

It should be obvious that complete accuracy in interpreting the meanings that are shared by people is rare, if not impossible. Such a level of accuracy would require symbols to be understood by the participants in *exactly* the same way. Further, even if complete understanding is possible in a given instance, it would be impossible to verify that the meanings that are created for the symbols are identical in the minds of all participants.

There are different levels or degrees of understanding. Communication requires a degree of understanding sufficient to accomplish the purposes of the participants, which can vary from one experience to another. For example, it may or may not be communication if a man, who is dressed in unfamiliar clothes and who is obviously from another culture, walks up to you and, after bowing, utters some sounds that seem like they could be language but whose meaning is unknown to you. If his purpose is merely to provide you with a **ritualistic** greeting and, recognizing this, you return his bow, relative to the purpose of the participants. In such a context, the two partners have created shared meanings because both of their behaviors are mutually understandable and consequently communication has occurred. However, if he is asking you for directions and you merely return his bow without even recognizing his intended goal, then shared meanings do not exist and communication has not taken place with regard to the task at hand.

5.3.3 Transactional

All participants in the communication process usually work together to create and sustain the meanings that develop. When people communicate, they are **simultaneously** sending and receiving messages at every instant that they are involved in conversation. The receivers provide the senders with ongoing responses about how the messages are received.

A communication is a two-way process. The goal of communication is not merely to influence and persuade others but also to improve one's knowledge, to seek understanding, to develop agreements, and to negotiate shared meanings. At any given instant, no one is just sending or just receiving messages, and therefore there are no such **entities** as pure senders or pure receivers. Nor does it make sense to describe a single message as being the **exclusive** one at any selected moment.

Rather, all participants are simultaneously interpreting multiple messages at every moment. These messages include not only the meanings of the words that are **articulate**d but also the meanings conveyed by the tone of voice, the types of gestures, the frequency of body movements, the motion of the eyes, the distances between people, the formality of the language, the seating arrangements, the clothing worn, the length of pauses, the words not articulated, and much more. Thus, in the transactional view it is impossible to describe one person as exclusively the sender and the other as exclusively the receiver. The participants in the transactional view are simultaneously senders and receivers.

5.3.4 Contextual

That all communication takes place within a setting or situation is called a context. Context means the place where people meet, the social purpose for being together, and the nature of the relationship. Thus, context includes the physical, social, and interpersonal settings within which messages are exchanged.

The Physical Context

The physical context includes the actual location of the interactants. It influences the communication process in many obvious ways. An afternoon conversation at a crowded sidewalk café and an evening of candlelight dining in a private salon will differ in the kinds of topics that are covered and in the interpretations that are made about the meanings of certain phrases or glances. If people know the physical context well, they can predict with a high degree of accuracy of communication. For example, people may place their romantic communications in a quiet, dimly-lit restaurant or on a

secluded beach. It is noticeable that knowledge of the physical context often provides important information about the meanings that are intended and the kinds of communication that are possible.

The Social Context

The social context refers to the widely shared expectations people have about the kinds of interactions that normally should occur within different kinds of social events. For example, communication at funerals differs from that at an office party. The social context of a classroom makes people expect certain forms of communication that differ from those at a soccer game. However, occasionally there may be a great deal of difficulties in understanding the social contexts for communicative events that involve other cultures, as the common expectations about what behaviors are preferred or prohibited may be very different. For instance, in Ireland, an all-night celebration called a wake before a funeral is sometimes held. Such behaviors, which are appropriate to the social context of an Irish funeral, would be completely inappropriate to other societies on the same occasions.

The Interpersonal Context

The interpersonal context refers to the expectations people have about the behaviors of others as a result of differences in the relationships between them. Communication between teachers and students, even outside the classroom context, differs from communication between close friends. Communication among friends differs from communication among acquaintances, co-workers, or family members. As people get to know each other and develop shared experiences, the nature of their interpersonal relationships is altered. This change in the interpersonal context is accompanied by alterations in the kinds of messages created and in the interpretations made about the meanings of the messages exchanged.

5.3.5 Dynamic

Communication is a dynamic process. Communication is an ongoing activity. The term 'dynamic process' conveys the idea that the two parties constantly shift their roles from encoders to decoders and exchange messages in each turn of interactional process.

In the process of communication, both parties are parts of the dynamic process of communication. They are constantly affected by the other's messages. Communication is like a motion picture, not a single **snapshot**. A word or action does not stay frozen. It is immediately replaced with another word or action.

Communication events are unique, as seemingly identical experiences can take on vastly different meanings at different stages of the process. This stream of events, which involves both past experiences and future expectations, is always moving and changing. Thus, the very same message may be interpreted rather differently when said at different stages of the communication process.

5.4 Communication Apprehension and Barriers

People begin to communicate at birth and continue communicating throughout their lives. Many people experience fear and anxiety when communicating with others, particularly in situations such as public speaking, class presentations, the first date, or a job interview. The fear people experience when communicating with others is called Communication **Apprehension**. For many years, the effects of Communication Apprehension have been concerned by many experts. It is noted that the highly communication-apprehensive person is very likely to fail to share many of the benefits in interaction. Furthermore, it has been established that people suffering from communication apprehension also behave differently in small group communication contexts. More recent research has confirmed the negative impact of communication apprehension on interpersonal attraction and on perceived **credibility**. In order to make communications effective, efforts must be directed toward helping people overcome this problem in especially public speaking courses. So, it is necessary to take into consideration the following barriers in communication system.

5.4.1 Language Barriers

If participants in intercultural interactions use different languages and vocabularies while communicating with one another, they probably don't understand each other, especially when they use their dialects with unique accents which represent national or regional barriers. Language barrier includes words having similar pronunciation but multiple meanings, badly expressed messages, wrong interpretations and unqualified assumptions, etc. The use of difficult, inappropriate words or misunderstood messages can result in confusion. As a result, people confronting such cases may experience communication apprehension.

5.4.2 Cultural Barriers

Cultural barriers include a great number of factors as culture itself is a very complex phenomenon. For example, one's age, education, gender, social status, economic position, cultural background, health, beauty, popularity, religion, political belief, ethics, values, motives, assumptions, **aspirations**, regulations, standards, priorities, etc can separate one person from another and create a communicative barrier. People are greatly influenced by the community culture they are living in. Different cultures provide people with different beliefs, values, norms, and ways of thinking. Thus when people from different cultures communicate with each other, cultural barriers probably come up.

5.4.3 Individual Barriers

Individual barriers may be a result of an individual's perceptual and personal discomfort. Even when two people have experienced the same event, their mental perception may/may not be identical with regart to what acts as a barrier. Style, selective perception, **halo** effect, poor attention and retention, defensiveness, close mindedness, insufficient filtration are the individual or psychological barriers. It is evident that the high apprehensions are closely related to individual barriers.

5.4.4 Interpersonal Barriers

Every person is a unique one with his or her filter of life experience. So the interpretation of the intended meanings in communication is greatly different because of interpersonal barriers. The common causes leading to interpersonal barriers are: limited vocabulary, emotional outbursts, communication selectivity, poor listening skills, noise in the channel and cultural variation. In companies for example, interpersonal barriers consist of two parts. One refers to barriers from the employers: lack of trust in employees; lack of knowledge of non-verbal clues like facial expressions, body language, gestures, postures, eye contact; different experiences; shortage of time for employees; no consideration for employees' needs; wish to capture authority; fear of losing power of control; **bypassing** and informational overloading, etc. The other is about barriers from employees: lack of motivation, lack of cooperation, trust; fear of penalty and poor relationship with the employer. In many cases, most employees experience communication apprehension to some degrees during the course of interacting with their employers. Of course, interpersonal barriers probably occur to family members, friends, relatives and colleagues even in daily communication.

5.4.5 Channel Barriers

Channel barriers are closely related to the means by which messages are transmitted. If the length of the communication is a little bit longer, or the medium selected is inappropriate, the communication might break up; it can also be a result of the interpersonal conflicts between the sender and receiver; lack of interest to communicate. Shared information may be another issue since there might be discrepancies in what is considered as shared things, and consequently, it will affect the clarity and accuracy. Nevertheless, access problems pose big problems for communication as well, which can seriously **hamper** the channel and effectiveness of the communication. Communication apprehension will arise because of various kinds of channel barriers. In fact, all people experience communication apprehension on some occasions. To experience communication apprehension does not mean they are abnormal or sick. In daily intercultural interactions, people should try to get rid of those barriers in order to be capable of adapting themselves in different circumstances. People may make greater efforts to overcome communication apprehension by getting to know some specific details in different communicative styles and mastering some important communication skills to be effective communicators.

5.5 Communicative Styles

Communicative styles refer to the ways in which language works to embody the user's communicative intentions. Researchers have identified numerous differences in communication styles from culture to culture. The direct and indirect communication styles are accepted as the common styles that can reveal the different communicative features of individualistic and collectivistic cultures.

5.5.1 Direct Communicative Style

People using a direct communicative style generally employ **overt** expressions of intention. By means of using a direct style, interactants assert self-face needs. Such messages clearly articulate the speaker's desires and needs. People say what they mean and mean what they say. People don't need to read between the lines. It's important to tell what it is, honesty is the best policy. The truth is more important than sparing someone's feelings.

The direct style is often used in low-context, individualistic cultures and preferred in such countries as the United States, England, Australia, Germany, and Canada. In low-context circumstances, people care less about others and, they prefer independence, self-reliance, and a greater emotional distance from each other. As a result, it is highly necessary for people to say what is on their mind frankly and directly. Because of the cultural values of precision, Americans tend to use explicit words such as "for sure," "no question," "without a doubt." Because of their low-context orientation, Americans tend to verbalize the messages to make their intentions clear and explicit. Americans are encouraged to "speak their mind." Words are the primary means of communication, while nonverbal cues are not the key to understanding. They are so direct that they might say in public like "I'll be right back," "I have to use the restroom." Direct communication style emphasizes facts rather than face. So getting or giving information is the **overriding** goal of the communication exchange. Criticism is straightforward, and it's okay to say no directly to people.

5.5.2 Indirect Communicative Style

An indirect communicative style, which is often seen in high-context and collectivistic cultures, is one where the speakers' intentions are hidden or hinted during interaction. The use of ambiguity and vagueness is characteristic of an indirect style. In high-context cultures, there is no need to articulate every message. Understatement is valued. True understanding is implicit, coming not from words but from actions in the context. Moreover, indirect communication prevents potentially embarrassing moments that might threaten the face of either speaker. Maintaining harmony is the overriding goal of the communication exchange. Confrontation is avoided, saying no is avoided, and criticism is handled very delicately. What one says and what one feels are often different.

The use of an indirect style of communication is seen in many Asian cultures. Chinese and Japanese speakers, for example, limit themselves to implicit and even ambiguous use of words such as "maybe" and "perhaps." Children in Japan are taught not to be self-centered, and those who take the initiative are generally not rewarded. Japanese mothers typically use **rhetorical** questions and tone of voice and context to express disapproval. There is a belief among Japanese that verbalizing deep feelings spoils their value. To the Japanese, being understood without words is far more cherished than precise articulation. In Japan, interpersonal communication is based on a great deal of guessing and reading between the lines. Directness is disagreeable and **repugnant**. The ability to correctly grasp what a person thinks and feels without verbal expressions is considered a sign of closeness between two persons.

Considerable differences between direct and indirect communication styles can be easily seen. Direct communication mainly relies on words, to be exact, relies more on literally interpreting those words and less on manipulating the context. Indirect communication owes much to the importance in preserving harmony and saving face which are extremely valued by many cultures. Variations of communicative styles may exist in any culture.

5.6 Communication Skills

Communication skills require message skills, interaction management, identity maintenance, and social skills. Message skills refer to the ability to select an appropriate behavior in diverse contexts. Interaction management means handling the procedural aspects of conversation, such as the ability to initiate a conversation. It emphasizes a person's other-oriented ability to interact, such as attentiveness and responsiveness. Social skills are **empathy** and identity maintenance. Empathy is the ability to think the same thoughts and feel the same emotions as the other person. Identity maintenance is the ability to maintain a counterpart's identity by communicating back an accurate understanding of that person's identity.

The following behavioral skills are suggested for effective interpersonal communication.

- ◇ Eye communication — to look sincerely and steadily at another person.
- ◇ Posture and movement — to stand tall and move naturally and easily.
- ◇ Gestures and facial expressions — to be relaxed and natural when speaking.
- ◇ Voice and vocal variety — to use voice as a rich, **resonant** instrument.
- ◇ Dress and appearance — to dress and appear appropriately in the context.
- ◇ Language, nonverbal, and pauses — to use appropriate and clear language, replacing nonverbal information with pauses.
- ◇ Listener involvements — to maintain the active interest and involvement of each person.
- ◇ Using humor — to create a bond among communicators.
- ◇ The natural self — to be **authentic**

The main purposes of communication are closely related to survival, co-operation, personal need, relationships, persuasion, power, social needs, giving or obtaining information, making sense of the world, and self-expression. Whether people manage others, products, services or any

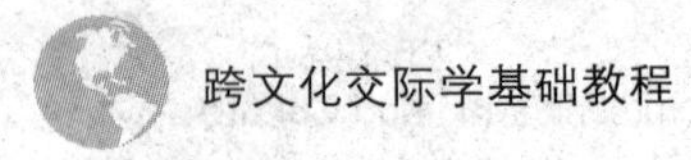

combination of these, they are all selling themselves through communication. Their success is determined by their ability to communicate — to persuade their listeners to react. And the ability to communicate effectively is dictated by how they are perceived by their listeners. Therefore, the greatest investment they can make is to develop their communication skills, to enhance their awareness of how they are perceived by others to achieve the effects they seek.

5.7 The Relationship between Culture and Communication

Hall (1959) holds that "culture is communication and communication is culture." It describes the relationship between culture and communication. We employ communication in every aspect of our daily life. Communication serves to facilitate human socialization, maintain social relationships, and develop personality. It is true that the development of human culture is made possible through communication, and it is through communication that culture is transmitted from one generation to another. We communicate the way we do because we grow up in a particular culture and learn its language, norms and rules. Culture and communication are intertwined.

Culture influences our communication in various aspects. Culture provides us with a system of knowledge that makes us know how to communicate with other members of our own culture and how to interpret their behavior. It affects how we interpret, perceive and respond to messages verbally and nonverbally. Culture shapes and colors our image of reality and conditions the way we think.

Culture **conditions** communication. Culture is the foundation of communication. Without the sharing and understanding between speakers, no communication is possible. Culture dictates every stage of communicative process. What we say, what gestures we use, with whom we talk, when and how to talk are all determined by our culture.

How we communicate and what is said through our communication help define what our culture is. Communication makes the development of culture possible. Culture is transmitted from one generation to another through communication. Culture is learned through communication. We acquire cultural patterns through socialization with other members of society. This socialization is realized by interacting with different social groups: friends, family members, teachers, peers, colleagues, etc. We learn our communicative behavior consciously from our parents, who teach us the norms and rules that guide our behaviors in our cultures. We learn how to compete and how to cooperate with others from our peers. We also learn about our cultures from the mass media. Television teaches us many of the daily norms and rules of our cultures and provides us with views of society. Without socialization through communication, the learning of culture is impossible.

Through communication and socialization, we may share certain common cultural characteristics but we may differ on other aspects. The similarities and differences are usually attributed to the beliefs and values embedded in such things as our history, tradition, education, religion and family structure. All of these beliefs and values are learned and passed down to different generations through a range of communication processes such as mass media, language, education, stories, folktales, mythology and proverbs.

In general, communication is an element of culture. Culture is a code we learn and share. Culture shapes our communication patterns. Communication, in turn, influences the structure of our culture. Communication can be understood only with the understanding of the culture that supports it.

New Words and Phrases

encode /ɪnˈkəʊd/ *vt*. 编码
decode /ˈdiːˈkəʊd/ *vt*. 解码
ingredient /ɪnˈgriːdɪənt/ *n*. 原料;因素
emblem /ˈembləm/ *n*. 标志,象征
obscene /əbˈsiːn/ *adj*. 淫猥的,下流的
arbitrary /ˈɑːbɪˌtrəri/ *adj*. 武断的
intrinsically /ɪnˈtrɪnsɪkəli/ *adv*. 本质的,内在的
episode /ˈepɪsəʊd/ *n*. 一集,一节
ritualistic /ˌrɪtjʊəlˈɪstɪk/ *adj*. 惯常的;(遵守)仪式的

simultaneously /ˌsaɪməlˈteɪnjəsli/ *adj*. 同时(发生或做出)的
entity /ˈentɪti/ *n*. 实体;实际存在物
exclusive /ɪksˈkluːsɪv/ *adj*. 独有(做或享)的
articulate /ɑːˈtɪkjʊlɪt/ *v*. 清楚地表达
seclude /sɪˈkluːd/ *v*. 使(自己或某人)与其他人隔离,使隐居
snapshot /ˈsnæpʃɒt/ *n*. 快照
apprehension /ˌæprɪˈhenʃən/ *n*. (对未来)忧虑,担心
credibility /ˌkredɪˈbɪlɪti/ *n*. 可靠性,可信性
aspiration /ˌæspəˈreɪʃən/ *n*. 志向,抱负
halo /ˈheɪləʊ/ *n*. (神像头上的)光轮;光晕
bypass /ˈbaɪˌpɑːs/ *vt*. 绕过,忽视
hamper /ˈhæmpə/ *v*. 阻碍,妨碍
overt /ˈəʊvɜːt/ *adj*. 明显的;公然的
overriding /ˌəʊvəˈraɪdɪŋ/ *adj*. 最重要的,压倒一切的
rhetorical /rɪˈtɒrɪkəl/ *adj*. 修辞的;与修辞有关的
repugnant /rɪˈpʌgnənt/ *adj*. 使人反感的,令人厌恶的
empathy /ˈempəθi/ *n*. 移情作用,同情
resonant /ˈrezənənt/ *adj*. 洪亮的;共鸣的
authentic /ɔːˈθentɪk/ *adj*. 可信的,真实的

Exercises

I. Questions for discussion

1. How is the process of communication achieved when people interact with one another?
2. In what ways can context influence human being's communication?
3. What is Communication Apprehension? And how do people overcome it?
4. What are the differences in Eastern and Western ways of expressing themselves?
5. How does culture influence communicative styles?

II. Comprehension check

Directions: *Decide whether the following statements are true* (*T*) *or false* (*F*)

________ 1. Communication comes from the Latin "communicare," which means, "to make common" or "to share."

_______ 2. All communication processes consist of ten components.

_______ 3. Feedback refers to the receivers' verbal message to the source.

_______ 4. Context could be as small as a classroom or a dinner table, and at the same time it could be as big as the entire cultural environment.

_______ 5. A sigh or frown accompanying speech, if noticed by the receiver, may also carry unintended messages to the receiver.

_______ 6. A man who is confident enough may avoid communication apprehension.

_______ 7. How People relate to one another will determine both the form and content of communication.

_______ 8. Different patterns of thinking will lead to different styles in communication.

III. Fill in the blanks with the words given in the bank

community	apprehension	styles	explicit	indirect
decoding	respond	interpretive	information	source

Communication is a process in which all parties involved convey information to one another. Once a __(1)__ originates the interaction, by means of the __(2)__ process together with the influence of other factors, a receiver may __(3)__ to the sender appropriately. But, in many cases, the communication does not go very smoothly because it is a very complex process. Being symbolic, __(4)__, transactional, contextual and dynamic are the most distinctive features of communication. Sometimes it's hard to interpret all the __(5)__ accurately in different cultural contexts. What's more, the dynamic feature of communication adds to the difficulties in understanding mutually in intercultural communication. Sometimes the more you know a person, the harder you can read him or her. Almost everyone experiences communication __(6)__ more or less in especially public interaction, so it's necessary to have a better understanding of the different communication __(7)__ between the East and the West. For example, westerners prefer clear, ___(8)___ and direct way of communication, while easterners like to talk in a vague, implicit and ___(9)___ way. Of course, for many people, to develop the communication skills in successfully interacting with others is becoming increasingly important. Every man or woman is deeply influenced by the ___(10)___ culture one lives in every moment. So, communication is culture and culture is communication.

Case Study

Case I

The following dialogue takes place between a young couple who have dated for a short time. The man is a U. S. student, and the woman is from Japan.

Jim: You know, Michiko, I really enjoy the time we spend together. I really like you. I've been so happy since we met.

Michiko: Hmmm, thank you.

Jim: I mean, I feel like I've learned so much about you and your culture.

Michiko: Yeah ...

Jim: I'm so glad you came to the United States. Do you like it here? What is your favorite thing about us?

Michiko: Well, it's pretty big. It's nice here.

Jim: What do you think about Americans?

Michiko: I don't know. Maybe I haven't been here long enough to know.

Jim: You must think something!

Michiko: Well, I'd probably have to think about it.

Jim: I mean, do you like us?

Michiko: Well, I don't really know about many Americans yet.

Adapted from Storti, C. (1994). *Cross-Cultural Dialogues: 74 Brief Encounters With Cultural Difference*. Yarmouth, ME: Intercultural Press

Questions for Discussion

1. What kind of communication style does Jim employ in the dialogue?
2. Describe the distinctive features of Michiko's communication mode.
3. How does the dialogue go between them in your mind?

Case Analysis

Americans tend to verbalize the messages to make their intentions direct, clear, explicit and easy to read. While Japanese prefer expressing themselves in an indirect, vague, implicit and hidden way. So Americans lay emphasis on making meanings clear in the verbal code and rely less on nonverbal meanings, whereas Japanese place importance on the interdependence between meaning and nonverbal code.

In all likelihood, Jim is not going to get much of a direct answer from Michiko. She continues throughout the dialogue using rather general answers to Jim's very specific and direct questions about her feelings toward the United States. Michiko might believe that Jim is being far too direct and invading her privacy. Michiko cannot possibly say something critical about the United States because she would lose face, as would Jim, as native. Therefore, she gives imprecise and indefinite answers.

Case II

It was a hot day. Since it was still too early to use the air-conditioner, according to the regulations of the university, every class kept its door open to make the classroom cooler. While I was lecturing on Chinese grammar in Class 4, waves of laughter came from the neighboring Class 5.

A German student named Stephen raised his hand and stood up. "The laughter from Class 5 is bothering us. I think we should go to their class to protest," he said.

His deskmate, a student from Japan, shook his head. "Is it necessary to protest over such a minor issue? I can tolerate this noise. And there are some Japanese friends of mine in Class 5. I don't want to make my friends unhappy just because of your protest."

Another Japanese girl stood up, "Let me close our door. Although that will make it hotter, it will be quieter."

She was stopped by a French student. "Why should we close our door and suffer from the heat? Class 5 should close their door in order not to bother other classes."

A few students from Africa suggested, "Why not strike our desks like drums to protest?"

A girl from Russia agreed, "Our class could also laugh together to let them know what the noise sounds like."

Two Korean students whispered to each other, "Western students really have a hot temper. They just don't know how to stay calm. How could we get along well with other classes if we can't control ourselves?"

A Hungarian girl happened to overhear their comments. She disagreed, "I don't understand you Asians. You won't protest even when your rights have been violated."

More laughter came from Class 5. Stephen stood up, "No matter what you think about it, I'm going to protest." He went to Class 5 and asked, "How happy you must be today! May we share in your happiness?" Laughter stopped. After a while, Class 5 closed their door.

Stephen came back satisfied and told his Japanese classmates, "Now you Asians can enjoy the peace won by us Westerners." After class, a few European students from Class 5 came to apologize to me. They said that they weren't aware that their laughter might have bothered Class 4. The Japanese students from Class 5, however, adopted a Chinese nickname for Stephen "*Jin jin ji jiao*" (people who haggle over every ounce).

Adapted from Fan Weiwei. (2010). *A Multimedia Approach to Intercultural Communication*. High Education Press.

Questions for Discussion

1. What bothered Class 4 on a hot day?
2. How many different solutions did Class 4 propose?
3. Why did a few European students of Class 5 make an apology to the teacher after class?

Case Analysis

Generally, Asian people are very courteous and indirect in their communication. Because they put great emphasis on group harmony, they are very tolerant, even when they are offended. These collectivistic values, shaped by Confucian teachings, were spread from China to many Asian countries. While Westerners are generally very direct and frank in their mode of communication. And they have a strong sense of protecting their own rights. Individualistic values are the underlying principles governing their behavior.

As the German student Stephen and his classmates from western countries demonstrate in the case, it is easy to see their clear, direct and explicit expressions to protect their own rights. Individualistic values are primary in their mind. While, the students from Japan and Korea think that the laughter from class 5 is just a minor issue, it is not necessary to protest. They can reduce the noise by closing their door and try to get along well with other classes. They regard harmony as fundamentality in interpersonal relationship.

Reading I

American and Japanese Conversational Patterns

Let's assume that people seem to play tennis while engaged in a conversation in America. In the game, the players start on opposite sides of the net. One player is designated the server, and the opposing player is the receiver. Service alternates game by game between the two players. For each point, the server starts behind their baseline, between the center mark and the sideline. The receiver may start anywhere on their side of the net. When the receiver is ready, the server will serve, although the receiver must play to the pace of the server.

An American-style conversation between two people is like a game of tennis. If I originate a topic, you are expected to hit it back simultaneously. If you agree with me, in most cases I expect you to add something — a reason for agreement, another example, or an elaboration to carry the idea further, of course I don't expect you simply to agree with me. I will be happy if you can question, challenge, or even completely disagree with me. Whether you agree or disagree, your response is to show your idea to me in the same way you hit back the ball.

And then it is my turn again. I don't serve a new ball from my original starting line. I hit your ball back again from where it has bounced. That means I carry your idea further, or answer your question or objections, or challenge or question you. And so the ball goes back and forth, an original spin, a powerful smash.

If there are more than two people in the conversation, then it is like doubles in tennis, or like volleyball. There's no waiting in line. Whoever nearest and quickest will hit the ball, if you step back, someone else will hit it. No one stops the game to give you a turn. You are responsible for taking your own turn . . .

A Japanese-style conversation, however, is not at all like playing tennis or playing volleyball, it is like bowling. When you are engaged in the game of bowling, you will select your bowling ball, line yourself up and wait for your turn to throw. And you always know your place clearly in line. While in Japanese-style of conversation, your turn of speaking depends on such things as whether you are older or younger, you are a close friend or a relative stranger to the previous speaker, you are in a senior or junior position, and so on.

In bowling, when your turn comes, you step up to the starting line with your bowling ball, and carefully throw it. Everyone else stands back and watches politely murmuring encouragement. Everyone waits until the ball has reached the end of the alley, and watches to see if it knocks down all the pins, or only some of them, or none of them. There is a pause while everyone registers your score.

Then, after everyone is sure that you have completely finished your turn, the next person in line steps up to the same starting line, with a different ball. He does not return your ball, and he does not begin from where your ball stopped. There is no back and forth at all. All the balls run parallel. And there is always a suitable pause between turns. There is no rush for the bowling. So do Japanese people in their conversation.

In terms of conversation, quite different from Americans, Japanese value silence. As members of the Japanese culture emphasize group harmony and believe that one's feelings cannot be conveyed through talk. In other words, these differences can be associated with the dimension of individualism versus collectivism. This negative attitude towards talk in Japan also accounts for the unfocused and fragmented nature of Japanese conversation. Many pauses and uncertainty can be noticed in Japanese conversation. When one is talking, others listen to him especially attentively, no interruptions can be found.

Reading II

Ten Tips for Acquiring Effective Communication Skills

By Elizabeth Scott, M. S.

In daily communication, we should pay much attention to the following ten skills for acquiring effective interpersonal communication.

Stay focused

Sometimes it's tempting to bring up the past seemingly related conflicts when dealing with current ones. Unfortunately, this often clouds the issue being discussed and makes finding mutual understanding to the current issue less likely, as well as makes the whole discussion more taxing and even confusing. So in most cases, the best way to solve the conflicts is trying not to bring up past hurts or other topics. Just stay focused on the present, our feelings, understanding one another and finding a solution.

Listen carefully

When we talk with people, we often think they are listening. In fact, they might as well be actually wondering what we are going to say next. Truly effective communication goes both ways. Try really to listen to what our partner is saying, don't interrupt, don't get defensive. Listen to them attentively and reflect back what they're saying, so they know we've listened carefully. Then we'll understand them better and they'll be more willing to listen to us. To some extent, listen carefully to each other is not only some form of mutual respect, but also is a necessity for attaining the final goal in communication.

Try to see their point of view

In a conflict, most of us primarily want to be heard and understood. We talk a lot about our point of view to get the other person to see things in our way. Ironically, if we all do this all the time, there will be little focus on the other person's point of view, and nobody feels being understood. If the interaction goes on and on in such a mode, no conflicts can be settled in the end. So try to really see the other side, and then we can better explain ours. Others will be more likely willing to listen to us if they feel they have been heard. Once both parties reasonably and carefully take into consideration the other's point of view, conflicts will be easily solved.

Respond to criticism with empathy

When others come at us with criticism, it is easy to feel that they are wrong, and at once we will get defensive. Generally criticism is hard to hear, and often exaggerated or colored by others' emotions. It is important to listen to others' pain and respond with empathy for their feelings. After all, we are looking for what is true in what they are saying as to get valuable information for us. Only in this way, can we see clearly our weakness and strength so as to make the communication move in favor of us smoothly.

Own what is ours

We must realize that personal responsibility is a strength, not a weakness. Effective communication involves admitting when we're wrong. If we bravely take on some responsibility in a conflict (which is usually the case), honestly look for and admit to what's ours. We'd better set a good example and show maturity as well as build the image of confidence. It also inspires others to respond in a similar way in most cases, leading us both closer to mutual understanding and a solution. The willingness to shoulder the responsibility from any party engaging in a conflict is the indispensable contribution to effective communication.

Use "I" messages

Rather than saying things like, "You really messed up here," we should begin statements with "I". For example, "I feel frustrated when this happens." In the same circumstance, using "I" message instead of the above "You" statement to express our frustration even anger is to make others feel less awkward. It is evident that "I" message is less accusatory, and sparks less defensiveness, and more importantly, helps others understand our point of view rather than feeling attacked. The result is the conflict is less tense even there is one.

Look for compromise

Instead of trying to 'win' the argument, look for solutions that meet everybody's needs. Either through compromise or a new solution that gives us both what we want most, sometimes even through a third party. This focus is much more effective than one person getting what he wants at the other's expenses. Healthy communication involves finding a resolution that both sides can be happy with. Meanwhile, effective communication means achieving the greatest interest through the cooperation even the compromise from both parties.

Take a time-out

Sometimes when tempers get heated, it may be too difficult to continue a discussion without it becoming an argument or a fight. What kinds of interacting means are appropriate for both parties? If we feel ourselves or our partners starting to get too angry to be constructive, or showing some destructive communication patterns, it is all right to take a break from the discussion until we both cool off. Sometimes good communication means knowing when to take a break.

Don't give up

Sometimes taking a break from the discussion is a good idea. If we both approach the situation with a constructive attitude, mutual respect, and a willingness to see the other's point of view or at least find a solution, we can make progress toward the goal of a resolution to the conflict. Unless it's time to give up on the relationship, don't casually give up on mutual purposes in communication. Stick to communicating with those who may not at the beginning share the same idea with us, and make great efforts to reach the agreement as possible as we can in communication.

Ask for help if we need it

If one or both of us has trouble staying respectful during conflict, or if we've tried resolving conflict with our partner on our own and the situation just doesn't seem to be improved, we might consult some relevant experts and benefit from a few sessions with a therapist. For example, couples counseling or family therapy can provide help to resolve future conflicts in families. We can also seek help from our friends by regularly meeting them. Sometimes the suggestions or advice from experts or friends are very useful in promoting better understanding among conflicting parties.

Adapted from http://stress.about.com/od/relationships/ht/healthycomm.htm.

Chapter Six

Language and Culture

Objectives

- Understand the nature of language.
- Learn the characteristics of language.
- Learn the mechanism of language.
- Understand the roles of language in culture.
- Understand the influence of culture on language.

导读

语言作为文化的重要组成部分，是文化的载体。作为一个有着语音、词汇、语义、句法等多个层面的复杂体系，语言具有任意性、符号性、创造性和动态性的特征。同时，语言与文化息息相关：人们通过语言传承文化，记录历史，并表达自己的文化认同；同时文化也在语言的词汇、意义、使用等层面留下深深的烙印。掌握语言中的文化因素是跨文化交际能力的一种体现。

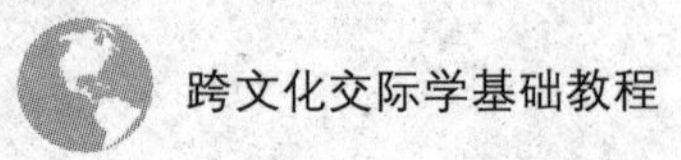

Text

6.1 The Nature of Human Language

We live in a world of language. We talk to our friends, our colleagues, our teachers, our parents, and even our enemies. We talk face-to-face or over the telephone. Such technological inventions as television and radio further swell this **torrent** of words. Hardly a moment of our waking lives is free from words, and even in our dreams we talk and are talked to. Apart from talking, language also allows us to understand or disagree with others, to make plans, to remember the past, to imagine future events, and to describe and evaluate objects and experiences that exist in some other location.

Though it penetrates into nearly every aspect of our lives, language is often taken for granted. We seldom realize its existence unless it hinders our communication. However, it is the possession of language, perhaps more than any other property, that distinguishes humans from other animals. To understand our human nature, we must understand the nature of language that makes us human.

6.2 The Mechanism of Human Language

Language is defined as a system of arbitrary vocal symbols used for human communication. It is a complicated entity with multiple layers and facets, so it is hardly possible to explore its mechanism all at once. Therefore, the exploration of language mechanism is concentrated on one aspect at a time. This has given rise to a number of relative independent branches.

6.2.1 Sounds of Language

As a vehicle for communication, language has two media: spoken and written forms. The spoken form of language consists of a systematic set of sounds combined with a set of rules. The production of these sounds involves the movement of airflow. Apart from the ability to articulate sounds, we are equipped with amazing ability to distinguish the differences in sound from the continuity of speech, and differentiate which **attributes** of the sound are of **linguistic** significance and which are not. For instance, if one coughs in the middle of saying "How (cough) are you?" a listener will ignore the cough and interpret the sound of cough simply as "How are you?" Men's voices are generally lower in pitch than women's. Some people speak slowly, while others speak quickly. These differences in speaking are not linguistically important.

6.2.2 Words of Language

Every speaker of every language knows tens of thousands of words. Word is an important part of our linguistic knowledge and we learn new words throughout our lives. Without words we would be unable to convey our thoughts through language.

Language is dynamic and there are new words regularly added to language. However, the coinage of new words is subjected to principles. We are going to use English examples to present some major principles by which new words are coined.

Compound word is formed by two or more words combined together. The ways in which words are combined in English are nearly limitless. Nouns can be combined with nouns, such as "boyfriend," "textbook," adjectives with nouns, such as "greenhouse," "blackboard."

Acronym is a word composed of the first letters of the words in a phrase, especially when this is used as a name. There are two types: word acronyms and spelling acronyms. Word acronyms are pronounced as ordinary words, not as spellings: **NATO** from "North Atlantic Treaty Organization", and AIDS from "acquired immune deficiency syndrome". Spelling acronyms are read and pronounced as spellings, as a sequence of letters. Examples are: IT from "information technology," VIP from "very important person" and UN from "United Nations."

6.2.3 Sentence Patterns of Language

Though any speaker of a language is capable of producing an infinite number of sentences, sentences are not formed at random. Instead, the sentence structure of any language is governed by the rules and principles. The order of words in a sentence and how the words are grouped are determined by syntactic rules which contribute to part of our knowledge of language. For instance, the words in the sentence "The dog ate the bone" can be grouped into (the dog) and (ate the bone), corresponding to the subject and predicate of the sentence. The sentence can be further divided as (the dog) (ate (the bone)), and the final division gives the individual words: ((the) (dog)) ((ate) ((the) (bone))). The structure of this sentence can be more clearly analyzed in a tree diagram:

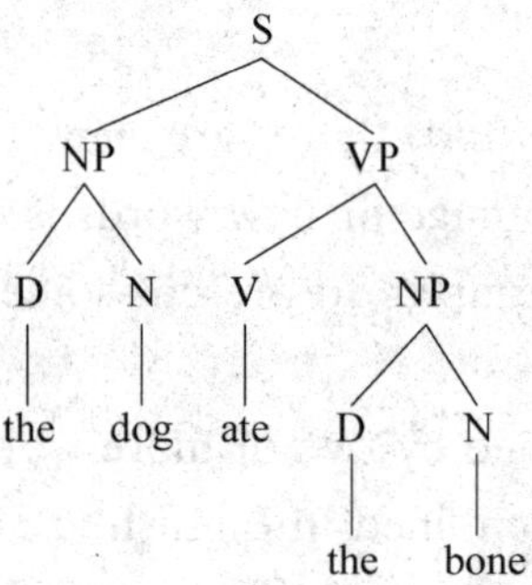

6.2.4 Meanings of Language

Words are the basic units of meaning. Understanding the meanings of words is, therefore, critical to the sharing of meanings conveyed in verbal communication.

Meanings stored in our minds do not exist in isolation. On the contrary, meanings are related to one another in a variety of ways. **Synonymy** and **antonymy** are examples of how meanings are related.

Synonymy refers to the sameness or close similarity of meaning. Words with the same or nearly the same meaning are called synonyms. However, it has been said that there are no perfect synonyms. Due to their different origins, there are often subtle differences between synonyms. They may differ in style, the degree of formality, such as the difference among "kid", "child" and "offspring".

Antonymy refers to the oppositeness in meaning, and words that are opposite in meaning are called antonyms. There are several kinds of antonymy. There are **complementary** pairs, e. g. alive/dead, and male/female. They are complementary in that "not alive" = "dead" and "not dead"="alive", and so on. There are also gradable pairs of antonyms: big/small, and hot/cold. They are gradable because the negative of one word is not the synonym of the other. For example, "not hot" does not necessarily mean "cold". Another kind of antonyms includes husband/wife, father/son etc. They are called relational opposite, for they display **symmetry** in their meaning: if X is Y's "husband", then Y is X's "wife".

6.2.5 Use of Language

The process of communication is essentially a process of conveying and understanding the intended meaning in a certain context. In everyday life, we may encounter situations when the literal meaning does not correspond to the intention.

The sentence "Is this your pen?" is used by Jiang Wangqi (2000) to illustrate the **asymmetry** between literal meaning and intended meaning. The literal meaning of this sentence is a question concerning the ownership of a pen. In actual situation, however, it may have several different meanings. When it is used in a post office by someone to a stranger beside, it may serve as a request, meaning "May I use this pen?" When it is used by a teacher to a student leaving the classroom after the class, it may function as a reminder, meaning "Don't leave it behind." And when it is used by a mother to a child, especially if the pen is on the floor, it may be intended as a command like "Pick it up!"

As the example indicates, such elements as knowledge of who is speaking, who is listening, and the situation in which communication takes place, will lead to different understanding of the same utterance. These components constitute what is identified as situational context. Situational context determines the speaker's use of language and also the hearer's interpretation of what is said to him.

Apart from situational context, there is another kind of context named cultural context, which also exerts great influence on how language is said and interpreted. An obvious example comes from people's appreciation of humor in different cultures. Whether a joke is judged as funny or not largely depends on the context where people have grown up. A Frenchman, for instance, might find it hard to laugh at a Russian joke. In the same way, a Russian might fail to see anything amusing in a joke which would make an Englishman laugh to tears.

6.3 The Characteristics of Human Language

To have a better understanding of language, we need recognize the defining characteristics of human language that distinguish it from any animal system of communication. In this section, we will discuss four characteristics of human language, namely, symbolic, creative, **arbitrary**, and dynamic.

6.3.1 Language is Symbolic

Language can be simply defined as a sign system. Pierce (1903) recognized three types of signs which differ according to the three types of relationship that exist between form and meaning: **icon**, **index**, and symbol.

An icon is a sign whose form has actual characteristics of its meaning. The icon resembles or imitates its object. See the two examples of iconic signs below. The first means "bus," and the second "raining." These two signs can have the meanings "bus", and "raining" respectively, since the forms have actual characteristics of these meanings.

Figure 6.1 bus

Figure 6.2 rainy

An index is a sign that denotes its meaning by virtue of an actual connection involving them. See the two examples of indexical signs below. The first example is a **skull** and crossed bones, which is traditionally a sign meaning "poison." The indexical and natural relation between the form and its meaning goes like this: "If you drink what is inside, you will look like this." The second sign, when seen posted at the side of a highway, will suggest "food service," because of the natural association between spoons and forks with food service.

Figure 6.3 poison

Figure 6.4 food service

A symbol is a sign that denotes its meaning solely by virtue of the fact that it will be interpreted to do so. That is, the symbol is arbitrarily associated with its meaning. Language consists of a system of symbols. Symbols in language are words that stand for or represent a unit of meaning. For example, we use the symbol "rice" to represent something that can satisfy physical hunger. When we are really hungry, of course we don't eat the symbol "r-i-c-e" but the real steamed or boiled grain.

6.3.2 Language is Creative

Language is creative in that it makes possible the construction and interpretation of new sentences. We have to rely on knowledge of a language to know and understand new sentences, for new sentences never spoken or heard before cannot be stored in our memory. For every sentence in the language, if a longer sentence can be formed, then there is no limit to the length of any sentence and therefore no limit to the number of sentences. For instance:

The movie is interesting.

The movie I saw is interesting.

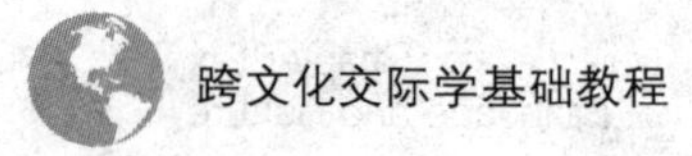

The movie I saw yesterday is interesting.

All human languages permit their speakers to form indefinitely long sentences, and creativity is a universal property of human language. Most animal communication systems appear to be highly restricted with respect to the number of different signals that their users can send and receive. For instance, the bees' dance is used only to indicate the location of food.

6.3.3 Language is Arbitrary

The arbitrary nature of language is closely related to the symbolic nature of language. By arbitrary, we mean that there is no **intrinsic** connection between a linguistic symbol and what the symbol stands for. The fact that different languages have different words for the same thing is a good illustration of the arbitrary nature of language.

Another good example accounting for the arbitrary nature of language is the fact that different sounds are used to refer to the same object in different language. The sounds represented by the letter "hand" signify the concept . In Chinese, the same meaning is represented by *shou*, *main* in French, *ruka* in Russian. The sounds of words are given meaning only by the language in which they occur.

However, we should be aware that although language is arbitrary by nature, it is not entirely arbitrary. Langacker (1987) argues that the arbitrary character of language is overstated. Many linguistic symbols are motivated rather than arbitrary. The most convenient example explaining the non-arbitrary nature of language comes from **onomatopoeic** words in almost all the languages, like "buzz" or "murmur" that imitate the sounds associated with the objects or actions they refer to.

6.3.4 Language is Dynamic

All living languages change through time. They have to constantly evolve in response to changing historical and social conditions. Language changes can occur in each layer of language: sound, word, grammar, meaning, and use.

To better illustrate the dynamic feature of language, we may use changes in the meanings of words as an example. Changes in meaning are realized through three processes, namely, widening, narrowing, and shift in meaning.

When the meaning of a word becomes broader, that word means everything it used to mean, and then more. For instance, the word "holiday," derived from "holy day," originally referred to a day which is religiously important. Today the word signifies any day on which people do not have to work.

The meaning of words can also be narrowed down over time. In the course of several generations, change has narrowed the meaning of a word to its current meaning. The word "deer" once meant "beast" or "animal". The meaning of "deer" has now been narrowed to a particular kind of animal.

The last type of changes in meaning is the shift in meaning. The word "nice" now generally means "pleasing, agreeable, polite, and kind." In the 15th century, however, it meant "foolish, and even wicked."

6.4 The Relationship between Language and Culture

Language and culture are so closely **intertwined** that it is extremely difficult to separate the two. On the one hand, language, as an essential part of human being, permeates our thinking and way of viewing the world. Language both expresses and embodies cultural reality. On the other hand, language, as a product of culture, is heavily influenced by culture, and the impact of culture upon a given language is something intrinsic and **indispensable**. Language in use is heavily tinted with its culture and the changes in language uses reflect the cultural changes.

6.4.1 The Role of Language in Culture

As is indicated above, language is an essential part of culture, and plays an important role in expressing cultural reality and embodying cultural identity. Samovar & Porter (2004) make the following summarization to highlight the role of language in culture:

6.4.1.1 Recording History

Language functions to record facts, a function represented by all kinds of record keeping, ranging from historical records, geographical surveys, and business accounts to scientific reports, legislative acts, and public-record data banks. This arena is an essential domain of language because the material guarantees the knowledge-base of subsequent generations which is a prerequisite of social development and the perpetuation of culture.

6.4.1.2 Transmitting Culture

While human capacity for language has genetic basis, for example, we were all born with the ability to acquire language, the details of any language system are not genetically transmitted, but instead have to be taught and learned. Language, as a vehicle for transporting information and ideas, takes on the major responsibility of transmitting culture. Like any vehicle, language is a medium for getting from one place to another. And like any vehicle, language can be improved on, made more efficient and effective, and fueled with high-quality material. And like any vehicle, language is seen primarily for its role in transmitting culture from one person to another, from one place to another, and from one generation to the next generation.

6.4.1.3 Expression of Identity

Culture helps supply a great deal of our identity. Much of this definition of our identity is reflected in the language we use. The verbal expression of identity unites participants in addition to presenting information. Cheering at a football game, or shouting names or slogans at public meetings can reveal a great deal about people and their identity — in particular their culture, regional origins, social background, occupation, age, sex, and personality.

Beyond shouting slogans or cheers, language functions to express and maintain our social identities. What you are can be very important in the eyes of society. Our sociolinguistic identities derive from the way in which people are organized into hierarchically ordered social groups or classes. The way people talk reveals a great deal about their social positions and their level of education.

6.4.2 The Influence of Culture on Language

As an indispensable part of culture, language is closely intertwined with culture, and is inevitably influenced by culture. We are going to explore the influences that culture exerts on language from such perspectives as word, meaning, and language use.

6.4.2.1 Influence of Culture on Word

It is widely accepted that language affects thought and culture. Many researches and experiments have lent support to the claim that people tend to sort out and distinguish experiences differently according to the semantic categories provided by their different languages. Generally speaking, people learn to name what is practical, useful and important. The more important the things appear to people, the more detailed they are categorized and named. As a result, the important things take on specific names while the less important things have general names that must be modified through additional words to become specific.

In this sense, culture actually exerts great influence on the way people create words. Each culture creates certain words to describe its unique physical and social environments as well as the activities its people engage in those contexts. Therefore, the absence of certain objects, events, concepts in one culture will naturally result in the absence of the necessary vocabulary to refer to them. A good illustration comes from the word "snow" in Eskimo and English. The Eskimos have countless words for snow in that snow is so crucial to life that each of its various forms and conditions is named. In English-speaking cultures, snow is far less important and the simple word "snow" usually suffices the needs. When some needs for specific terms arise, longer phrases can be made up to meet these needs, such as "corn snow," "drifting snow." This phenomenon was first notice by Franz Boas in his *The Handbook of North American Indians* (1911):

> Just as English uses derived terms for a variety of forms of water (liquid, lake, river, brook, rain, dew, wave, foam) that might be formed by derivational morphology [suffixes and other such stuff] from a single root meaning "water" in some other language, so Eskimo uses the apparently distinct roots aput "snow on the ground", gana "falling snow", piqsirpoq "drifting snow", and qimuqsuq "a snow drift".

Another example to illustrate the influence of culture on word can be found in how kinship relations are described in different cultures. Different cultures classify kinship relations differently and therefore use different systems to describe these relations. Chinese kinship system is one of the most complicated of all kinship systems, where kinship relations are described based on such parameters as generation, relative age, gender, etc. As a result, one's father is distinguished from one's father's brother and from one's mother's brother. One's mother is similarly distinguished from one's sister and from one's father's sister. For cousins, there are eight possible terms in Chinese.

6.4.2.2 Influence of Culture on Meaning

In order to illustrate the culture' influence on meaning, we need make the distinction between **denotative** and **connotative** meanings. Denotative meanings are the public, objective, and legal meanings of a word. They are the primary, explicit meanings given in a dictionary. Connotative meanings are the implicit, supplementary value which is added to the purely denotative meanings of a word or phrase. They are personal, emotionally charged, private, and specific to a particular person. For instance, the denotative meaning of the word "rose" is a kind of flower. But at the same time, it also triggers many associations, mostly good ones such as love, fragrance, passion and beauty.

The same word in different languages may have different connotations. For example, due to cultural differences, "apple" in English is endowed more connotations than it is in Chinese. Therefore, there are more English expressions and proverbs with apple than in Chinese:

Adam's apple: a body part at the front of the neck

Rotten apple: a single bad person or thing

Upset the applecart: to ruin plans or arrangements

The apple of one's eye: special favorite, beloved person or thing

The apple never falls far from the tree: The children will usually turn out like the parents.

Conversely, there are words which have more connotative meanings in Chinese than they do in English. For instance, wild goose, which means nothing more than a common bird in English culture, is endowed a poetic sense in Chinese culture. There are numerous poems and idioms concerning wild goose in Chinese: "*yan zi hui shi*, *yue man xi lou*", "*chen yu luo yan*", etc.

Difference in connotative meanings may also impose difficulty on intercultural communication. Since connotative meanings are culture-bound, words with same denotative meanings may differ in connotative meanings. As the proverb "as timid as a hare" shows, English culture uses "hare" to compare timid people. By contrast, in Chinese culture, people choose another animal "mouse" to connote the same meaning. Then the proverb is better translated into Chinese as "*dan xiao ru shu*" or "*dan xiao ru tu*"? Similarly, "tiger" represent king of animals in Chinese culture, while English language chooses "lion" to carry the same connotative meaning. The proverb in English "beard the lion in his den" is thus translated into Chinese as "*hu kou ba ya*".

In general, language symbolizes cultural reality. Language is a system of signs that is seen as having itself a cultural value. Speakers identify themselves and others through their use of language; they view their language as a symbol of their social identity. So language symbolizes cultural reality.

It is concluded that the interplay between language and culture creates infinite possibilities that can enrich our human experience, expand our vision of the universe, and promote understanding among people with different language and cultural systems.

New Words and Phrases

torrent /ˈtɒrənt/ *n*. 奔流,爆发
attribute /əˈtrɪbjuːt/ *n*. 属性
linguistic /lɪŋˈgʊɪstɪk/ *adj*. 语言的;语言学的
compound word 复合词
acronym 首字母缩略词
NATO /ˈneɪtəʊ/ 北大西洋公约组织
synonymy 同义关系

antonymy 反义关系
complementary /ˌkɒmplɪˈmentəri/ *adj*. 互补的;补充的
symmetry /ˈsɪmɪtri/ *n*. 对称;整齐
asymmetry /əˈsɪmɪtri/ *adj*. 不对称的,不对等的
arbitrary /ˈɑːbɪtrəri/ *adj*. 随意的,任性的
icon /ˈaɪkɒn/ *n*. 图标,图符
index /ˈɪndeks/ *n*. 指示;标志
skull /skʌl/ *n*. 颅骨,头盖骨
intrinsic /ɪnˈtrɪnsɪk/ *adj*. 本质的,固有的
intertwine /ˌɪntəˈtwaɪn/ *v*. 纠缠
indispensable /ˌɪndɪsˈpensəbl/ *adj*.不可缺少的;责无旁贷的
denotative /dɪˈnəʊtətɪv/ *adj*. 指示的,外延的
connotative /ˈkɒnəʊteɪtɪv/ *adj*. 含蓄的
onomatopoeic /ˌɑnəˌmætəˈpiːɪk/ *adj*. 拟声的;声喻的

Exercises

I. Questions for discussion

1. Can you use an example to explain the point that "meaning resides in context"?
2. In what sense is language dynamic?
3. Can you use examples to explain the roles language plays in culture?
4. Can you use examples to explain how culture influence language?

II. Comprehension check

Directions: *Decide whether the following statements are true* (*T*) *or false* (*F*).

_______ 1. There are some many words describing kinship in Chinese in that kinship is highly emphasized in Chinese culture.

_______ 2. NATO is an acronym, which is coined by combining the first letters of the words in a phrase.

_______ 3. Language is entirely arbitrary, and there is no intrinsic connection between a linguistic symbol and what the symbol stands for.

_______ 4. The speaker's intention is often conveyed indirectly and has to be inferred by the hearer in relation to the context.

_______ 5. Due to their different origins, there are often subtle differences between synonyms.

_______ 6. Language permeates all aspects of our life so that we are quite conscious of its existence.

_______ 7. Denotative meaning is heavily tinted by cultures and refer to the emotional associations that a word or phrase suggests in one's mind.

_______ 8. Speakers identify themselves and others through their use of language; they view their language as a symbol of their social identity.

III. Fill in the blanks with the words given in the bank

complicated	symbolic	context	rule-governed	dynamic
creative	intertwined	reality	imitate	mould

Though bees can communicate effectively and parrots can ___(1)___ human language vocally, language is peculiar to human beings. Human language has several features that distinguish it from other communicative systems used by animals. In the first place, language is ___(2)___. The sounds and words used in a language are viewed as symbols. These symbols and meanings they refer to have no necessary logical relation, which is the arbitrary feature of language. Besides symbolic and arbitrary features, language is ___(3)___, which makes possible the construction of numerous new sentences which we may never have heard or spoken before. No matter what amount of sentences we may create, these sentences are subjected to rules and principles. In this sense, language is ___(4)___. In addition, language is ___(5)___. That is, language changes over time, and there are new words and phrases constantly added to language and old ones are gradually abandoned.

The complexity of human language also distinguishes it from other communicative systems used by animals. Human language is a ___(6)___ entity with multiple layers and facets: sounds, words, meanings, and use in ___(7)___. Language and culture are closely ___(8)___. In the first place, without knowledge of cultural context, meaning cannot be created or interpreted through language. Secondly, language is used to ___(9)___ new meaning and modify convention. Thirdly, language is a key influence in intercultural communication. Finally, language symbolizes cultural ___(10)___.

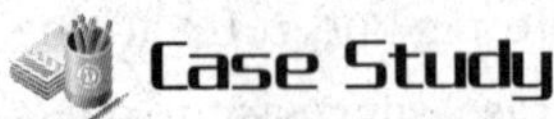

Case I

Professor Tulai, an American linguist, and professor Yang, a visiting scholar from China, are talking about the relationship between teaching and doing research in the office.

Prof. Tulai: To do research means to get your hands dirty.

Prof. Yang: So you think teaching is worthier than doing research? Does the phrase "to get your hands dirty" have some pejorative connotation?

Prof. Tulai: Oh, no! I didn't mean that. When I was saying that, I simply meant "you are practicing something," or "you are engaged in doing something."

Questions for Discussion

1. What is the literal meaning of "to get your hands dirty"?
2. What is the idiomatic meaning of "to get your hands dirty"?
3. When you encounter a phrase with similar idiomatic meanings, what strategy will you take?

Case Analysis

"To get your hands dirty" has to be understood idiomatically. When you get your hands dirty, it does not necessarily mean in the American culture that you've done some manual work and need to wash your hands. Instead, it means that you become involved in something where the realities might compromise your principles. It can also mean that a person is not just stuck in an ivory tower dictating strategy, but is prepared to put in the effort and hard work to make the details actually happen.

Such phrases as "to get your hands dirty" are termed idioms. By idiom, we mean an expression, word, or phrase that has a figurative meaning that is comprehended in regard to a common use of that expression which is separate from the literal meaning or definition of the words. There are estimated to be at least 25, 000 idiomatic expressions in the English language. Literal translation of these idioms will not convey the same meaning in other languages. For instance, a listener knowing only the meanings of "kick" and "bucket" would be unable to deduce the true meaning of the idiom "to kick the bucket." Idioms tend to confuse those unfamiliar with them; students of a new language must learn its idiomatic expressions as vocabulary.

Case II

The following is a situation we often encounter in China or see in Chinese films. When Spring Festival comes, people would hold a large party at home to celebrate the coming of New Year with family members. Lots of delicious foods are made. Children play games happily. On these occasions, parents would warn children not to break any cups or glass items, for it is regarded as bad luck to break something on Spring Festival. However, if children break cups or glasses owing to carelessness, parents usually would not blame them. Since sounds will be made when the cups or glasses fall down on the ground, parents then say "sui sui ping an," which means being safe and sound with the coming of the new year. The phonemes of "break" and "year" are the same, all pronounced as "sui" in Chinese. In fact, the morphological meaning is quite different. Chinese people are smart to change a negative case into a positive one. The positive linguistic concepts such as being safe and sound in the coming year can be considered as good luck attributes.

This is an example of how the Chinese employ language to reverse bad luck. The unfortunate incident of breaking an object is transformed to a fortunate incident when a person orally uses a positive expression to describe the unfortunate act. By examining the speaking pattern, it is possible to understand how Chinese people "play" with words and their meanings through the use of implied statements that represent a positive idea.

Questions for Discussion

1. In what way is the utterance "sui sui ping an" related to the action of

breaking something?

2. What are the possible reasons for people using language to reverse bad luck?
3. Can you figure out other examples when people use words with positive meaning to express something embarrassing to them?

Case Analysis

In all cultures, there are acts that are forbidden or to be avoided, and those acts are the so-called taboos. When an act is taboo, reference to this act may also become taboo. That is, first people are forbidden to do something, and then they are forbidden to talk about it. Forbidden acts or words reflect the particular customs and views of the society. Some words may be used in certain circumstances and not in others. In this case, "sui" which means "to break" becomes a taboo only when it is Spring Festival.

The existence of taboo words and ideas stimulates the creation of euphemisms. A euphemism is a word or phrase that replaces a taboo word or serves to avoid frightening or unpleasant subjects. For instance, in many societies death is feared and there are a number of euphemisms related to this subject. People are less apt to "die" and more apt to "pass away".

In this case, "sui" is a taboo word when Spring Festival comes, for "to break something" on Spring Festival is feared to bring bad luck and is to be avoided by Chinese. The worry about bad luck stimulates the usage of euphemism "sui sui ping an." The clever utilization of homonym has successfully relieved the unpleasant situation.

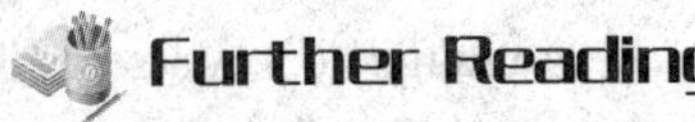

Further Reading

Reading I

Colors: Their Connotations and Perceived Meanings

Jeanette Joy Fisher

Throughout the ages, colors have been used to evoke certain emotions, and an examination of the history of color offers fascinating insights into the human condition, as well as shows how different cultures have developed different attitudes about color. Here are a few examples of what various colors have come to represent over the years.

Red

Red has traditionally been associated with courage and love in Western culture, but in China, red is the color of happiness and good fortune. White has traditionally been the color most preferred for wedding dresses in America, while the Chinese prefer to dress their brides in red.

Orange

Orange is considered a warm color, perhaps because it has evoked the feeling of fire, all the way back to mankind's earliest beginnings. Painting walls a subtle orange, leaning toward a warm brown, stimulates the appetite and can reduce tension. However, as the orange color becomes brighter, it begins to take on a high energy feel and can lead to anxiety.

Brown

Brown is another warm and comforting color, stimulating the appetite and actually making food taste better. That makes coffee brown, in all **intensities**, with or without the cream, an ideal candidate for dining rooms.

Yellow

Since it's always been associated with the sun, yellow has traditionally been considered a cheerful color. Yellow is also the first color most people see in early spring, when the **daffodils** begin to bloom. However, there seems to be an East/West cultural difference when it comes to yellow. The Chinese have revered yellow enough to have considered it the imperial color since the 10th century, yet several Western studies have shown that yellow is many people's least favorite color.

Green

Green is another color that has both an up and down side. It's associated with the new growth of spring, prosperity, and clean, fresh air, yet it can also carry a negative connotation, in terms of mold, **nausea**, and jealousy. Throughout the ages, green has most often been considered to represent fertility, and during the 15th century, green was the most popular choice of color for the wedding gowns of European brides.

Blue

Because it's associated with the color of the sea and the sky, blue has come to symbolize **serenity** and infinity. That's especially true of the more greenish shades of blue, such as aqua and teal. On the other hand, cooler shades of blue can have a tendency to cause feelings of sadness.

Purple

Over the millennia, purple has been associated with royalty in Western civilizations, due to the difficulty and expense involved in producing purple dye, which was made from a particular species of **mollusk shell**. Even today, when purple can be produced just as inexpensively as any other color, the use of purple is still considered to represent elegance and **sophistication**.

There are stories and connotations for every color, and different cultures assign different meanings to colors. For instance, American brides generally prefer white wedding dresses, while many Asian cultures dress their brides in black, reserving white for funerals. But regardless of what culture it is, one thing is certain: colors will always have effects on human beings and should be carefully considered when decorating a home.

Adapted from http://EzineArticles.com/? expert=Jeanette_Joy_Fisher.

Reading II

Taboo and Euphemism

Taboo generally describes the thing which cannot be mentioned because it is either too sacred, like the name of God, or too offensive, like sex. **Freud** reminds us, in *Totem and Taboo* that "Taboo is a **Polynesian** word, the translation of which provides difficulties for us because we no longer possess the idea which it connotes" (1950, 18). Historically, taboos have tended to move from religious to secular, especially sexual to racial, topics, but they can manifest themselves in relation to a wide variety of things, creatures, human experiences, conditions, deeds, and words. Strictly speaking, a taboo action should not be performed nor referred to, and a taboo word should never be uttered.

Taboo is a borrowed word which originally refers to acts that are forbidden or to be avoided. However, the notion of prohibition is not new and can be found in all societies. Originally spelled *tabu* in the Melanesian languages, the word had a complex social and anthropological meaning: when used as an adjective, it described physical locations that were sacred, set apart for gods, kings, priests, or chiefs, and therefore prohibited for general use. Cook notes in his account that "the word has a very comprehensive meaning; but, in general, signifies that a thing is forbidden." It could also be used as a verb: Cook records that a man had "been discovered with a woman who was tabooed." (Cook's description conforms to the taboos of his own time by not referring explicitly to sexual activity.)

Linguistically taboo is rooted in word magic, especially in the belief that certain forces and creatures cannot or must not be named. These have come to include a great range such as the name of God, the Devil, death, damnation, disease, madness, being crippled, the varieties of excretion, and copulation, and in some societies, being fired, being poor, being fat, having a humble occupation, or references to underclothes. Taboos can present themselves in unexpected forms. One of the strangest is that the Germanic ancestors of the English regarded the bear as a creature of such sacred force that it was referred to only indirectly as "the brown one" or "the honey wolf." In several religions, such as Islam, direct reference to the name of God is taboo. This is not the case with Christianity, although there are biblical **injunctions**, such as the Third Commandment, against "taking the Lord's name in vain."

Absolute taboos are rare and impractical, since they obviously hinder communication and cannot be enforced in an increasingly secular and multicultural world. Consequently, the relationship between taboo and **euphemism** is symbiotic. As the entry for euphemisms shows, some euphemisms are time-honored, such as those for the name of God, while others are comparatively recent, such as those relating to fatness. Historically, there are few areas of continuous taboo. In medieval times, contrary to expectation, the name of God was used very freely in ways, while "four-letter" words were used in certain literary genres and even in medical textbooks. In the Victorian era virtually all the categories listed in the previous paragraph were taboos. The exception was fatness, admired in the male **embonpoint**. Today taboo increasingly refers to prohibitions against socially unacceptable words, expressions, and topics, especially of a sexual and racist nature. They are also governed by context and medium, being most strictly observed in the press, the printed word, and broadcasting, but less so in oral usage, especially in male-to-male talk.

There are also biographical and individual factors governing taboos, especially that of age. Louis MacNeice explores this theme in *The Blasphemies*, a poem tracing changing sensitivity through decades of personal maturation. It begins with the child's speculation: "The sin against the Holy ... though what / He wondered was it?" "Cold in his bed," he is terrified at the prospect that "I shall be damned through thinking Damn." But ten years later he is "Preening himself as a gay blasphemer." "Rising thirty, he had decided / God was a mere expletive, a cheap one." Between forty and fifty "He grew to feel the issue irrelevant." The poem ends with the taboo broken, but the question remaining: "The sin / Against the Holy Ghost — What is it?"

In recent decades the notion of linguistic taboo has shifted from being actual to mythical. Revealingly, in the first linguistic instance given in the Oxford English Dictionary, Leonard Bloomfield writes in his classic study *Language* (1933): "In America knocked up is a tabu form for 'rendered pregnant'," thereby breaking the supposed taboo in an example that now seems rather strange. (In Victorian times even the word pregnant was taboo.) A double standard is particularly apparent in modern dictionaries, which commonly employ the usage label "taboo" of sexual and racist terms, even though these words are acknowledged to be in common use. The modern use of **corpora**, or large bodies of evidence of actual usage, both spoken and written, has enabled compilers of dictionary to make meaningful assessments of word frequency. These clearly show that the notion of "taboo" is misused. Thus the *Longman Dictionary of Contemporary English* (3rd edition, 1995) is based on both the Longman Corpus and the British National Corpus to establish the 3,000 most frequently used words in spoken and written English. Although fuck is marked as "taboo," its usage is rated as S3, one of 3 000 most frequently spoken words — while fucking is rated even higher as S1, one of the 1 000 most frequently spoken words. Bastard, bugger, and bloody are rated as S3, while shit and ass are rated as S2. (None of these words achieves so high a rating in written usage, and the first three are far more common in British than in American English.) Furthermore, it should be noted that usage labels in modern dictionaries tend to be remarkable in their inconsistency.

The increasing use of taboo to mean simply "offensive" or "grossly impolite" rather than "strictly forbidden" is also apparent in recent publications actually using the term in their titles. These include *A Dictionary of Obscenity, Taboo and Euphemism* (1988) by James McDonald and *Forbidden American English* (1990) by Richard A. Spears. The latter often rates some words (e. g., fuck) as "taboo in all senses," but others (e. g., cunt) as merely "very vulgar." However, the work gives quite elaborate caution notes.

In recent decades, as taboos have moved from sexual to racial terms, the **lexicographical** accommodation of ethnic slurs has attracted much controversy. The Oxford University Press was subjected to protests and eventually a lawsuit in 1972 over the inclusion of **opprobrious** senses of the word Jew. Two years previously the editor in chief of *Webster's New World Dictionary* pointedly omitted what were termed in the Preface "those true obscenities, the terms of racial or ethnic opprobrium." Today, former taboos against religious exclamations are less stringently observed, while gross sexual terms are increasingly current. What is considered to be the most genuine taboo is that of race.

Adapted from http://encyclopedia.jrank.org/articles/pages/822/Taboo.html.

Chapter Seven

Nonverbal Communication and Culture

● **Objectives**

➢ Understand the nature of nonverbal communication.

➢ Understand the characteristics of nonverbal communication.

➢ Understand the types of nonverbal communication.

➢ Understand the functions of nonverbal communication.

➢ Understand the relationship between nonverbal communication and culture.

● **导读**

非语言交际是交际者运用身体的自然特征和本能向对方传递信息，表达特定语意的过程，如身体动作、面部表情、空间利用、触摸行为、声音暗示、穿着打扮和其他装饰等，甚至包括没有表情的表情、没有动作的动作。美国心理学家 Albert Mehrabia 通过实验证实：信息的总效果＝7％的文字＋38％的音调＋55％的面部表情和动作。这就是说“我们用发音器官说话，但我们用整个身体交谈。”

人类的非语言交际行为是在人类文化的制约下形成的，生活在不同文化环境中的人们的仪态举止和身势动作表现各异，而这些非语言行为又能反映其文化所给予的特定含义。作为文化的一部分，非语言交际的准则既是人类社会的自然过程，又是社会交往的产物。在非语言行为中，有的行为如体型、身高、某些面部表情、身势等，是本能的，具有自然性，而大多数行为则是后天学会的，具有社会性。

Text

7.1 Nature of Nonverbal Communication

All intentional and unintentional **stimuli** between communicating parties, other than the spoken words, are considered to be nonverbal communication. Some researchers abroad suggest that about 7% of the meaning in an interaction is conveyed by verbal communication while about 93% by nonverbal communication. Nonverbal actions constitute a second symbol system that enables people, even from different cultural backgrounds, to gain insight into our thoughts and feelings.

Nonverbal symbols include a wide range of behaviors such as body movements, postures, facial expressions, gestures, eye movements, physical appearance, the use and organization of space, the structuring of time, and vocal **nuances** etc. That is to say, everything from a nod to the wave of a hand, from wearing a new suit to arriving five minutes early for an appointment are all reflections of nonverbal communication. We all attempt at times to manage the impressions that others have of us. For example, we intentionally choose to wear certain clothes and groom in a certain way to show our best appearance and manner to leave a good impression on the employer when we are interviewed for a job. All of these activities and **artifacts** transmit meaning, thus are also considered to be nonverbal communication.

Much of nonverbal communication is unintentional and unconscious. Most people are not fully aware of nonverbal communication until they study it, which is why some scholars refer to it as a hidden dimension or a silent language. Culture to a large degree determines which posture, which gesture, or which interpersonal distance is appropriate in a host of social situations. In order to communicate effectively, it is particular important to become aware of nonverbal behaviors in different cultural contexts.

7.2 Characteristics of Nonverbal Communication

In interpersonal communication or intercultural communication, both verbal and nonverbal communication work in combination rather than isolation. Compared with verbal communication, nonverbal communication is a subtle, nonlinguistic, multidimensional, and **spontaneous** process. Without being able to use words, body gestures generally express our feelings and attitudes. People, both the senders and receivers, process nonverbal messages with less awareness than they process verbal messages. Nonverbal communication possesses three characteristics: it is less systematized; it is culture-bound; and it is ambiguous.

Nonverbal communication is less systematized and less precise than verbal communication. Unlike verbal languages that are grounded on a set of grammatical and comprehensible rules, there are no formal sets of rules to provide a systematic list of the meanings of a culture's nonverbal code systems. The meanings of nonverbal messages are usually less precise than those of verbal codes. It is difficult, for example, to define precisely the meaning of a raised eyebrow in a particular culture.

Nonverbal communication is culture-bound. Certain nonverbal messages, such as the V sign and the smile, can be used universally. But on other occasions, the same nonverbal message may convey various meanings across cultures. Even if some expressions of nonverbal behaviors are universal and governed by biological necessity, the meanings attached to these expressions show great variety across cultures. For example, while physical contact between a male and a female is a common practice of social greeting in western society, it is a taboo in some Asian cultures.

Nonverbal communication is dominated by ambiguity. Most of the nonverbal messages are continuous and natural, and they tend to blur into one another. The context in which the communication occurs, the relationship between the participants, the mood or feeling of the sender and receiver, will all affect the interpretation of the nonverbal behaviors. For example, to people of different cultures, a smile or a laugh may have very different meanings. In some eastern Asian countries, people do not readily show emotions. They are conditioned to use their face to conceal rather than reveal their feelings. The Japanese smile is not necessarily a spontaneous expression of amusement, but a law of **etiquette**, elaborated and cultivated from early times. In Africa, on the other hand, laughter is used by black people to express surprise, wonder, embarrassment and even **discomfiture**.

7.3 Types of Nonverbal Communication

Nonverbal communication is a rich, complex field of study. Unlike written or spoken words, nonverbal communication occurs in multiple channels simultaneously. The diverse types of nonverbal communication and the demonstration of importance in understanding how members of one culture attempt to understand, organize, and interpret the nonverbal behaviors of others are explored in this section.

7.3.1 Kinesics

The study of body movements is known as **kinesics**. Kinesic behaviors include gestures, head movements and other physical displays that can be used to communicate.

Although we possess both spoken and written languages, our conversations are full of nonverbal noises, gestures and facial expressions which not only enhance the actual words we utter but make them more efficient as well. For instance, when it is important that no one speaks, a whispered "sssssh" with a finger to the lips would demand silence far more effectively than a politely verbal request like, "Would you mind keeping quiet, please?"

Let's take hand gestures as examples to further explore kinesics. Hand gestures are considered significant in human interaction because they are so often used in social rituals and always responsible for a good first impression. For example, Westerners shake hands, Tanzanians clap hands ten times to

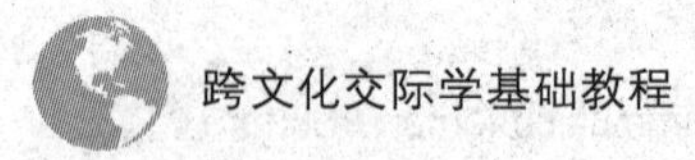

say hello, the Polish and Romanians kiss the back of the hand, Eskimos use hands to give a friendly punch on the head or shoulder, Thais and Indians put hands together in front of the face and slightly bow. As for some certain social rituals, Muslims and Hindus only use their right hands to pick up foods or to give an object to someone else. According to their religious belief, the left hand is considered unclean.

The best advice to people abroad is to keep your hands in your pockets, lest you be gravely misunderstood. Specifically, the once familiar hand gesture may mean differently even oppositely when we are in a totally foreign culture. For example, the thumb held upright with a closed fist has various meanings. In England and many countries today it is generally used to mean approval or success. To the Chinese it means "excellent" or "number one"; to the Japanese it represents boss, father, or husband; to North Americans it means "Okay" or "right on". And to people in the Middle East it is an **obscene** gesture.

And the "A-okay" sign can get you into all kinds of trouble too. To North Americans, it means everything is perfect. Yet this same gesture means money to Japanese. To the French, the ring sign shows that they think someone is a "zero," or "nothing." The same sign is also considered as an insult in Malta and Greece, and is perceived as an obscene gesture in Brazil. During World War II, British statesman Winston Churchill made his famous "V" for "Victory" sign to encourage his soldiers and people to fight against Hitler.

7.3.2 Oculesics

The study of communication sent by the eyes is known as **oculesics**. Shakespeare's "Your lips tell me no, but there is eye, yes in your eye" well describes the importance of eye contact in human communication.

Eye contact has different connotations in different cultural contexts. There are cultures in which direct eye contact between men and women is regarded as a sexual invitation and is, therefore, to be avoided in polite society. For example, in North America, it is rude for a man to gaze or stare at women. However, in Italy, men may gaze at women all the time and the women don't feel offended. People in the Middle East, especially Arabs, consider gazing as a way to show respect in communication.

People in individualistic cultures tend to engage in eye contact when listening to others more than when speaking. The listeners' eye contact is interpreted as an indication whether they are listening to the speaker attentively. Asian people tend to avoid eye contact when speaking and listening because they think that averting one's eyes may be a sign of respect, modesty or disinterest, rather than inattentiveness or submissiveness. While middle class Americans have a problem accepting this. As for them, looking down or away from the speaker means that the person is ignoring or rejecting what the speaker is saying. Therefore, the misinterpretation of the use of eye contact might cause serious misunderstanding in intercultural communication.

7.3.3 Haptics

The study of touch is known as **haptics**. Touch is often used to indicate affection, the expression of positive or negative feelings and emotions. Protection, reassurance, support, hatred, dislike, and disapproval are all conveyed through touch.

Touch can be used as a means of control and ritual purposes. Touching for control may indicate social dominance. High-status individuals, for example, are more likely to touch than to be touched. Touching for ritual purposes occurs mainly on occasions involving introductions or departures. Shaking hands, clasping shoulders, hugging, and kissing the checks or lips are all forms of greeting rituals.

Cultures differ in the overall amount of touching people prefer. These cultural differences may lead to difficulties in intercultural communication. Germans and Japanese, for example, may be perceived as cold and aloof by Brazilians and Italians, who in turn may be regarded as aggressive, pushy, and overly familiar by northern Europeans. In northern Europe one does not touch others. Even the brushing of the overcoat sleeve used to **elicit** an apology.

Cultures also differ in where people can be touched. In Thailand and

Malaysia, for example, the head is considered to be sacred and should not be touched because the **locus** of a person's spiritual and intellectual power is thought to be there.

Cultures vary in their expectations about who touches whom. Among the Chinese, shaking hands among people of the opposite sex is perfectly acceptable. For those who practice the Muslim religion, casual touching between members of the opposite sex is strictly forbidden. Holding hands or walking with an arm across someone's shoulder or around the waist, or even grabbing an elbow to help another cross the street, are all considered socially inappropriate behaviors between men and women. In some places, there are legal restrictions against public displays of hugging and kissing, even among married couples.

7.3.4 Proxemics

Proxemics refers to the study of how people differ in their use of personal space. Edward Hall (1966) coins the term and argues that people regulate intimacy by controlling sensory exposure through the use of interpersonal distance and space. He also suggests that people interact within four spatial zones or distance ranges: intimate, personal, social and public. In the United States, the proper social distance is about 4 - 12 feet. And the proper personal distance is about 1.5 - 4 feet. These proxemic zones are characterized by differences in the ways that people relate to one another and in the behaviors that typify the communication that will probably occur in them.

Personal space distances are culturally specific. Mexicans, for example, have a slightly smaller sphere of intimate space than North Americans. The result of this difference, which can be measured in just a few inches, is that when a North American and a Mexican stand together to converse, the Mexican will nudge slightly closer to the North American in order to get at the right distance for comfortable interpersonal discourse. The North American, who has a slightly larger intimate sphere, however, will feel that the Mexican is invading his or her intimate space and step back an inch or two. This will make the Mexican feel uncomfortable because he or she will feel too distant and, therefore, he or she will move closer.

Space affects human communication in many other aspects. For instance, whether or not individuals remain behind their desks when visitors enter their offices is an unstated message about friendliness or formality. Classroom arrangements of desks and chairs can determine how much discussion takes place in a class. A circular arrangement generally encourages discussion, while sitting in a row often discourages student participation. New communication technologies like the internet may overcome the` effect of spatial barriers whether two people are working in adjoining buildings or are located across the world from each other.

7.3.5 Chronemics

Chronemics is the study of how we perceive the concept of time and how it affects our communication. The **temporal** focus of human life can be directed on the past, the present, or the future.

The past orientation **predominate**s in cultures placing a high value on tradition. Past-oriented cultures regard previous experiences and events as most important. These cultures place a primary emphasis on tradition and wisdom passed down from the older generations. Innovation and change tend to be discouraged. When change is necessary, it should be justified by the past experience. In Saudi Arabia, any person who "changes" is presumed to be violating Muslim religion.

The present orientation predominates where people pay relatively little attention to what has gone in the past and what might happen in the future. Present-oriented cultures consider the present as the only precious moment. People should "let past pass!", "seize the day!" and enjoy today without worrying about what may happen tomorrow. Cultures such as those in the Philippines and many central and South American countries are usually present-oriented. They tend to be more impulsive and spontaneous and have a casual, relaxed lifestyle. They believe that unseen and even unknown outside forces, such as fate or luck, control their life. And they have found ways to encourage a rich appreciation for the simple pleasures that arise in daily activities.

The future-oriented cultures emphasize planning in order to achieve goals. Changes and innovations are encouraged in those cultures and are evaluated in terms of economic payoffs. As Hall (1994) puts it, "In the west, no one can escape the control of time. In fact, all social activities and business activities and even sexual life are controlled by time. Time weaves the net of one's life. Although people are unconscious of this, it decides and coordinates our life." Americans and others in the western world are said to live in the present and the near future so that they look upon time as a present, **tangible** commodity, something to be used, something to be held accountable for. They spend it, waste it, save it, divide it, just as if they are handling some tangible object. Americans also place great stress on **punctuality**. Any consistently tardy person is taken to be undependable, untrustworthy, and disrespectful.

7.3.6 Paralanguage

Paralanguage refers to the study of voice or the use of vocal signs in communication. It involves sounds but not words. The uhs, ahas, and uhms we use in our conversation are examples of paralanguage. Researchers classify paralinguistic cues into four categories: vocal qualities, vocal characterizers, vocal qualifiers, and vocal **segregate**s.

Voice quality seems to be more of an individual than a cultural characteristic because each individual has a distinctive voice quality. A person's voice may be shrill, **muffle**d, childish, or nasal, and another's can be breathy, **resonant**, or melodious, so culture does not affect the interpretation of voice quality much. But certain types of voice quality are still affected by cultural stereotypes. For example, North Americans tend to think a woman is discontented when she uses a **strident** and high-pitched voice and sexy when she uses a breathy and low-pitched voice.

Vocal characterizers are nonverbal voices that reveal our physical and emotional state. It is nearly universal for humans to laugh when they are happy; cry when they are in sorrow; yell (or be totally silent) when they are angry at someone; and yawn when they are tired. Vocal characterizers also include cues such as **belch**ing, groaning, hiccupping, moaning, sighing, sneezing, snoring and spitting.

Vocal qualifiers are variations of our voice that convey our emotions and personality. It refers to volume, pitch, and the overall intonation or "melody" of the spoken word. Each language system possesses its own acceptable range of vocal qualifiers. For example, in the Arab world speaking loudly signifies being strong and sincere, but such behavior may seem irritating and aggressive to North Americans.

Vocal segregates are those voice noises that seem not to serve any function but to interfere with the flow of speech. Examples include "um," "uh," "eh," "I mean" and "you know" in the middle of speaking. These words are called "fillers," simply for building a bridge to what the speaker says next. For example, most Japanese use *hai* as a filler without a particular meaning. It serves as a **lubricant** for the flow of the speech. In intercultural communication people must be aware of the appropriate frequency and meaning of fillers.

7.4 Functions of Nonverbal Communication

Nonverbal communication messages function as a "silent language" and transmit their meanings in subtle and **covert** ways. Communicators who do not share the same language may try to make themselves understood via gestures. In a very noisy manufacturing facility, communicators might use hand gestures to replace spoken messages. A police officer directing the flow of traffic uses nonverbal communication instead of verbal language for **utilitarian** purposes. Thus nonverbal messages allow us to show exactly what we wish to convey.

7.4.1 Expressing Emotions and Attitudes

Nonverbal messages can generally substitute for verbal messages to express people's emotions and attitudes, especially in situations in which words cannot communicate sufficiently what they mean. It is through nonverbal messages that we infer the feelings and attitudes of the stranger in the interaction. For instance, some messages are awkward or difficult to express in words without hurting feelings or making embarrassment. Imagine we are on our way home depressed due to failure in our final examination and are stopped by an acquaintance who wants to talk with us. The message in our mind is "Leave me alone." But we will not say those words because it will hurt our acquaintance, then we can express that meaning by looking gloomy and slowly walking away. Our nonverbal communication is received without bad feelings because it shows to them clearly that we do have to leave for something sorrowful.

Nonverbal communication may also **amplify** or tone down a verbal message to control other person's behaviors so that we may better express our interpersonal attitude. For example, when scolding someone, we often frown. Or stern eye contact from parents can stop the naughty behavior of children while guests are in the house. Hand clapping by the instructor in a classroom sounds **authoritative** and may demand the attention of the students. Or, if we want to moderate the verbal scolding, we may smile at the other person.

7.4.2 Reflecting and Managing Identities

Nonverbal messages serve as the markers of our identities. Whenever we come into contact with others, our sex, race, age, face, hair, clothing, body shape, and overall physical attractiveness are visually displayed and then interpreted through the **mediation** of **stereotypes** (Smith & Bond, 1993). Our accents, posture, and hand gestures tell others something about ourselves and how we want to be perceived, and further give our group membership away. For example, many devout Muslim women wear clothing that is at least ankle long and partially sleeved. They also veil their face wholly or partially in countries such as Saudi Arabia, Kuwait, the Arabia Gulf states, Yemen and Libya, as appropriate acknowledgement of the status and nature of women.

Furthermore, the uniforms that people wear also connote different identity markers. Uniforms in Japan, for example, worn by students, businessman, entertainers, and ever vacationers, among others, reflect the individual's special relationship to a specific identity group.

7.4.3 Conversational Management

People generally use their hand gestures, body postures, eye gaze or face gaze to manage their conversation with others. Hand gestures and body postures have been **categorized** as **emblems**. Every culture has a rich variety of emblems with specific meanings and rules of display. However, emblems can contribute to intercultural misunderstanding or conflicts. For example, the beckoning "come here" gesture observed in many Asian cultures (e.g., China and Japan) with the palm down and the fingers waving toward the body can signal "go away" to most North Americans.

Nonverbal communication can also regulate and manage our conversation with others. For example, a glance at our conversation partner may be important in signaling turn-taking. Professors delivering lectures in class can monitor the reactions of their students through their eye contact, body posture, and other nonverbal behaviors and adapt their lectures accordingly. Students who raise their hands in class are signaling the professor that they have questions or comments. Such behavior manages the flow of communication in the classroom. Individually, we can regulate the flow and pace of a conversation by engaging in direct eye contact, **affirmative** head nodding, and **stance**, thus signaling our conversational partner to continue or stop the communication.

7.4.4 Impression Formation and Attraction

When we manage our impressions on the nonverbal level, we are concerned with creating a favorable impression in the presence of others so that they can either be attracted to us or at least find us credible. Cultural values and norms influence the **implicit** criteria that we hold for in terms of perceiving other people as attractiveness or unattractiveness. In comparing U.S. and Japanese perceptions of attractiveness, U.S. college students have consistently rated smiling faces (both American and Japanese faces) as more attractive, intelligent, and sociable than neutral faces. Although the Japanese students have rated smiling faces as more sociable than neutral faces, they have evaluated neutral faces as more intelligent. Additionally,

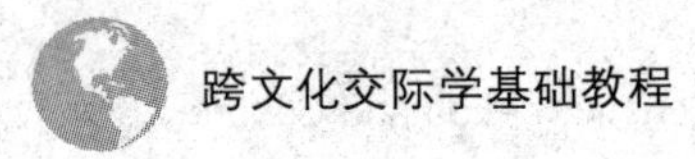

the Japanese students do not perceive smiling faces as being more attractive than neutral faces (Matsumoto & Kudoh, 1993).

In terms of the perceived credibility aspect, facial **composure** and body postures appear to influence our judgments of whether individuals appear to be credible or not credible. In some Asian cultures (e.g., South Korea and Japan), influential people tend to maintain restrained facial expressions and postural rigidity. In the U.S. culture, however, relaxed facial expressions and postures are associated with credibility and giving positive impressions.

7.5 The Relationship between Nonverbal Communication and Culture

Culture is all-pervasive, multidimensional, and boundless, it exists everywhere and in everything. Every culture has display rules that govern when and under what circumstances various nonverbal expressions are required, permitted, or prohibited.

Nonverbal communication is part of culture. It is shaped and influenced by culture, thus reflects culture. Hall (1966) refers to the largely unconscious phenomenon of nonverbal communication as the "hidden dimension" of culture. It is regarded as hidden because nonverbal messages are embedded in the contextual field of communication. Every culture has its own system of nonverbal behaviors. One's clothes and jewelry, the countless expressions he reflects with his face, the hundreds of movements he makes with his body, where and how he touches people, his gaze and eye contact, vocal behavior such as laughter, and his use of time, space, and silence are just some of the behavior in which one engages that serve as cultural messages.

Both culture and nonverbal behavior need to be learned. Although much of outward behavior is innate (such as smiling, moving, touching, eye contact), we are not born knowing the communication dimensions associated with nonverbal messages. Most scholars would agree that "cultures formulate display rules that dictate when, how, and with what consequences nonverbal expressions will be exhibited." To put in slightly different terms, we are born with the capacity to cry yet what makes us cry and who is allowed to see us cry need to be learned as part of cultural "education."

New Words and Phrases

stimulus /ˈstɪmjʊləs/ *n*. 刺激;刺激物
nuance /ˈnjuːˈɑːns/ *n*. 细微差别
artifact /ˈɑːtɪfækt/ *n*. 人工制品;手工艺品
spontaneous /spɒnˈteɪnɪəs/ *adj*. 自发的;自然的
etiquette /ˈetɪˈket/ *n*. 礼节,礼仪
discomfiture /dɪsˈkʌmfɪtʃə/ *n*. 狼狈;挫败
obscene /əbˈsiːn/ *adj*. 淫秽的,猥亵的
elicit /ɪˈlɪsɪt/ *vt*. 引出,引起
locus /ˈləʊkəs/ *n*. 场所;所在地
temporal /ˈtemp(ə)r(ə)l/ *adj*. 暂时的;当时的
predominate /prɪˈdɒmɪneɪt/ *vt*. 支配;主宰
tangible /ˈtændʒəbl/ *adj*. 有形的;可触摸的
punctuality /ˌpʌŋktjʊˈælɪti/ *n*. 严守时间
segregate /ˈsegrɪgeɪt/ *n*. 使隔离
muffle /ˈmʌf(ə)l/ *vt*. 抑制;发低沉的声音
resonant /ˈrez(ə)nənt/ *adj*. 洪亮的
strident /ˈstraɪd(ə)nt/ *adj*. 刺耳的;尖锐的
belch /beltʃ/ *vi*. 打嗝;喷出 *vt*. 打嗝;喷出
lubricant /ˈluːbrɪk(ə)nt/ *n*. 润滑剂;润滑油
covert /ˈkʌvət/ *adj*. 隐蔽的;隐秘的
utilitarian /ˌjuːtɪlɪˈteərɪən/ *adj*. 功利的,实用的
amplify /ˈæmplɪfai/ *v*. 扩大,详述
authoritative /əˈθɒrətetɪv/ *adj*. 有权威的;命令式的
mediation /miːdɪˈeɪʃ(ə)n/ *n*. 调解;仲裁
stereotype /ˈsterɪə(ʊ)taɪp/ *n*. 陈腔滥调;老套
categorize /ˈkætəgəˈraɪz/ *vt*. 分类
emblem 象征
affirmative /əˈfɜːmətɪv/ *adj*. 肯定的;积极的
stance /stɑːns; stæns/ *n*. 姿态
implicit /ɪmˈplɪsɪt/ *adj*. 含蓄的;暗示的
composure /kəmˈpəʊʒə/ *n*. 镇静;沉着

kinesics 形态学
oculesics 目态学
haptics 触觉学
proxemics 间距学
chronemics 时间学
paralanguage 副语言

Exercises

I. Questions for discussion

1. How do you communicate intimacy nonverbally?
2. Give examples to show how *kinesic* varies from one culture to another.
3. How does physical appearance affect first impressions during interaction?
4. What are the major differences between verbal and nonverbal communication?
5. Explain how culture and nonverbal behaviors interrelate to each other.

II. Multiple choice

Directions: Choose the best answer to each of the following questions.

1. Concerning paralanguage, ________ seem to be more of an individual than a cultural characteristic.

   A. vocal qualities　　B. vocal characterizers
   C. vocal qualifiers　　D. vocal segregates

2. Which of the following examples illustrates the function of reflecting and managing identities?

   A. Japanese students rating smiling faces as more sociable than neutral faces
   B. a police officer directing the flow of traffic
   C. parents stopping the naughty behavior of children with stern eye contact
   D. devout Muslim women wearing very conservative clothing

3. "It is difficult to define precisely the meaning of a raised eyebrow in a particular culture." The above expression is to show that nonverbal communication is ________.

   A. less conscious　　B. less systematized

C. culture-bound D. ambiguous

4. Edward Hall refers to the largely unconscious phenomenon of nonverbal communication as the "hidden dimension" of culture. It is regarded as hidden because nonverbal messages are embedded in the ________ field of communication.

   A. utilitarian B. social C. contextual D. covert

5. Which of the following doesn't belong to the future-oriented culture?

   A. to plan in order to achieve goals

   B. to be encouraged to seize the day

   C. to look upon time as tangible commodity

   D. to place great stress on punctuality.

III. Comprehension check

Directions: *Decide whether the following statements are true* (*T*) *or false* (*F*).

________ 1. Without being able to use words, body gestures can totally express our feelings and attitudes.

________ 2. Interpretation of the nonverbal behaviors will not be affected by the mood or feeling of the sender and receiver of the conversation.

________ 3. Certain nonverbal messages, such as the V sign and the smile, can be used universally. So a smiling face is a very safe nonverbal message throughout the whole world.

________ 4. We may use some nonverbal messages to amplify or tone down verbal messages to control other person's behaviors and to better express our interpersonal attitude.

________ 5. Specifically, the once familiar hand gesture may mean differently even oppositely when we are in a totally foreign culture.

________ 6. Innovation and change are not welcomed in both past-oriented culture and present-oriented culture.

________ 7. Acquired throughout the socialization process, nonverbal behaviors are mostly explicit and are processed cognitively.

________ 8. Some negative interpretations of strangers' nonverbal behaviors will decrease the effectiveness of our communication with them.

Case Study

Case I

Appropriate gazing behavior can have important consequences in certain communication situations. Consider the following communication exchanges between applicants for student visa to the United States and U. S. consular officers.

Scene 1:

Official A: You should look at me when you are speaking, and could you speak louder? I can't hear you. (*In a commanding voice*) How do you plan to pay for your tuition beyond the first year?

Applicant X: My uncle is going to be responsible (*Looking downward*).

Official A: Which is which? Your uncle or your father? (*In an accusatory manner*) You indicated earlier that your father is going to pay your way.

Now consider another visa applicant interview.

Scene 2:

Official B: I'd like you to look at me when you speak.

Applicant Y: Okay, sir. I'll try. (*The African visa applicant adjusts his behavior accordingly.*)

Official B: Who is responsible for paying your tuition?

Applicant Y: My uncle, Mr. Black.

Official B: So your uncle will be paying your tuition throughout your stay abroad.

Applicant Y: Yes, sir. There (*Pointing to a document in the official's hand*) is the affidavit from him.

Official B: What a nice uncle you must have.

Official B believes the second applicant is truthful and awards him a student visa to the United States. Applicant X's visa application is rejected.

Questions for Discussion

1. Explain why applicant Y is awarded visa application while applicant X is rejected?

2. What cultural implication does this case reveal?
3. What should you do if you want to communicate effectively with people from low-context culture?

Case Analysis

During this scenario, the applicants and consular officials are apparently from different cultural backgrounds. People in low-context cultures tend to engage in eye contact more often than individuals from high-context backgrounds where averting one's eyes may be seen as a sign of respect, modesty or disinterest.

Both the officials represent a low-context culture where status and power are believed to be relatively equal, and where direct eye contact is expected and is regarded as an indicator of truthfulness. That also explains why both official A and B asks the applicants to raise their voices and look at them when they answer questions.

The applicants are from a high-context culture in West Africa where individuals of lower status avoid direct eye contact with a superior. The failure in appropriate oculesics behavior leads to rejected visa application in scene one. Applicant X doesn't follow Official A's directions, such as raising his voice, making eye contact with him, answering the questions truthfully etc. While in scene two, Applicant Y adjusts timely to the situation and wins the student visa to the United Stated finally.

Case II

In the following two scenarios, Jim, Akira, and Mitsuko interact. Akira and Mitsuko are exchange students from Japan who are spending a semester studying at an American college. Jim is an American student at the same college. Notice how each violates the others' expectations without realizing it.

When reading the scenes, keep in mind the different cultural orientations and the assumptions of nonverbal expectancy violations theory.

(*Jim and Akira are at a party.*)

Jim: (*Nudges Akira and says loudly*) This is a great party, eh?

Akira: (*Startled, stands back and tries to put some distance between himself and Jim*) Yes, thank you.

Jim: (*Leading forward toward Akira, with direct eye contact*) If you want to meet some girls, I could introduce you.

Akira: (*Shocked by such an offer, he backs away*) But I don't know them. They might be upset.

Jim: Well, how else are you going to meet them?

Akira: (*Uncomfortable*) Maybe during a class or something.

(*Mitsuko, another Japanese exchange student, approaches Jim and Akira. She knows Akira, but not Jim.*)

Mitsuko: Hello, Akira. (*Bows slightly and looks down*)

Akira: Ah, Mitsuko, this is my friend Jim.

Jim: Hi! (*Forward leaning into her space*)

Mitsuko: Hi, Jim. (*Bows slightly and does not make direct eye contact*)

Jim: Are you two friends? (*Wonders why she won't look at him, thinks to himself, "Well, I'm not one of them. She probably thinks I'm ugly."*)

Akira: Yes, we know each other.

(*A long pause ensues.*)

Jim: (*Thinks to himself, "This is going nowhere — I've got to think of something to say." He speaks rather loudly*) Great party, hey guys?

(*Akira and Mitsuko both jump back.*)

Akira: (*Thinks to himself, "This guy is too weird"*) Yeah, this is fun.

Questions for Discussion

1. Why is Akira startled and shocked by Jim's behavior?
2. How would you explain Jim's behavior?
3. What cultural differences does this case reveal?

Case Analysis

In this scenario, Jim violats Akira's kinesic, proxemic, paralinguistic, and haptic expectations. In Line 1 when Jim touches Akira, he doesn't realize that he probably violates Akira's nonverbal expectations regarding haptics. In Lines 1 through 4, Akira perceives that Jim is standing too close, talking too loudly, so he backs away. From Akira's point of view, Jim violates his proxemic and paralinguistic expectations. From Jim's point,

Akira violates his expectations as well, because Akira doesn't look at him nor respond to his offer when he wants to introduce some girls to him.

In this dialogue, we can see how both Akira and Jim become startled, annoyed and uncomfortable by each other's violations. A Japanese studying in the United States, should change his behavior to conform to the expectations of others.

Adapted from "Intercultural Communication — A Contextual Approach by James W. Neuliep 2009 by SAGE Publications. Inc.

Further Reading

Reading I

Silence

Silence does not indicate action at first glance, yet communication through silence plays an important role in all cultures. The importance of silence as a communication tool and the interpretation of silence vary form culture to culture, but all cultures use silence at times to get a point across.

Hall uses silence as a basis for his division of low-context cultures and high-context cultures. "In low-context cultures in which ideas are encoded **explicitly**（明确地）into words, silence often is interpreted as the absence of communication. It is down time." While silence may hold strong, contextual meanings in high-context cultures, prolonged silence is often viewed as "empty pauses" or "ignorant lapse" in the Western rhetorical model. European Americans perceive the use of talk as being a means of social control, whereas native-born Chinese perceive the use of silence as being a conversational control strategy. Modern Chinese parents, on the other hand, use talk to create closeness and intimacy and silence to signal attentive listening and understanding.

As for Americans, Germans and other northern Europeans, they see silence in the process of vocal activities as a stop of communication and are uncomfortable with silence during conversations. In their eyes, silence indicates that the sender's words do not register with the receiver, or the receiver is not very happy with the current situation, or the receiver wants some more time to rethink the message etc. The sudden silence during a conversation might make people in low-context cultures wonder that the communication could have gong wrong.

Generally Speaking, silence is not a meaningful part of life of most members of the dominant culture in the United States. Talking, watching TV, listening to music, and other sound-producing activities keep them from silence. Compared with the American view of silence, people in high-context cultures, such as Japanese, Arabian, and **Mediterranean**（地中海）peoples, have a different attitude toward the use of silence. There is often a belief among many Eastern traditions that words can **contaminate**（污染,弄脏）an experience and that inner peace and wisdom come only through silence. They tend to have extensive information networks among family, friends, colleagues, and people who are involved in close personal relationships. For example, Japanese people pay a great deal of emphasis on silence. Silence is gold, and silence can speak more than words can do. Silence means differently in different situations. It could mean one is thinking about the matters being talked about. Or it means the speaker has not decided whether to speak or not. Even when the Japanese are threatened by others, they will choose silence as a **counterattack**（反击,反攻）.

In France, people tend to engage in animated conversations to affirm the nature of their established relationships; in the absence of such relationship, silence serves as a neutral communication process. That is why on the bus, in the street, or in the lift, people don't talk to each other readily in France. With strangers, the French generally preserve proper distance by means of silence. In contrast, European Americans tend to talk in order to "break the ice" and reserve silence for their most intimate relationship.

In addition, the use of silence is also a critical strategy in dealing with both in-group and out-group conflicts in collectivistic cultures. Silence can signal either approval or disapproval in collectivistic conflict interaction. Silence can be interpreted as an ambiguous "yes" or "no" response. In individualistic cultures, silence may well be viewed as an admission of guilt or a sign of incompetence.

Reading II

Posture and Sitting Habits

Posture and sitting habits offer insight into a culture's deep structure. In many Asian cultures, the bow is much more than a greeting. It signifies the culture's concern with status and rank. In Japan, for example, low posture is an indicator of respect. Although it appears simple to the outsider, the bowing ritual is actually rather complicated. The person who occupies the lower station begins the bow, and his or her bow must be deeper than the other person's. The superior, on the other hand, determines when the bowing is to end. When the participants are of equal rank, they begin the bow in the same manner and end at the same time.

The manner in which we sit also can communicate a message. In the United States, where "casualness" is considered a great virtue, people often sit with feet on chairs or even desks. They sometimes sit with their backsides (buttocks) on tables and desks as a free attitude. **Slumping**（下降）oneself over while sitting in a chair and placing feet on whatever object around is a common U. S. behavior. It is intended to show that the person is casual, honest, sincere, and "just one of the folks." In the United States, even millionaires, corporation presidents, government leaders and movie stars try to pretend they are ordinary people by using "the U. S. **slouch**（懒散的人，笨拙的人）" and "the feet-on-the-furniture" **maneuver**（调遣）.

Unfortunately, people of other countries may interpret this behavior as being **sloppy**（草率的，粗心的）and as reflecting a general lack of alertness, interest, and respect. Americans do not usually realize that what they think of as casualness is viewed very differently and very negatively by many people around the world. People in many cultures are expected to sit erect. Such cultures include many countries in Latin America, Asia, Europe, and the Middle East. For instance, in countries such as Germany and Sweden, where lifestyle tends to be more formal, slouching is considered a sign of rudeness and poor manners.

In the United States, crossing legs is a sign of good etiquette. Americans feel comfortable crossing their legs and sitting with one ankle on the other knee. Many cultures say that crossing legs is okay, but placing the ankle on the knee is totally unacceptable. You can cross your legs but not put your ankle on your knee in some Latin and Asian countries. In Peru, men can place the ankle on knee, but women must cross their entire legs at the knee. In Syria women must not cross their legs at the knee. In Ghana, and in Turkey, sitting with one's legs crossed is extremely offensive. People in Thailand believe that because the bottoms of the feet are the lowest part of the body, they should never be pointed in the direction of another person. In fact, for the Thai, the feet take on so much significance that people avoid **stomping**（跺脚，重踩）with them.

One reason for not putting the ankle on the knee is that when you do so, one foot or the sole of the shoe is usually pointing at someone. This is a very severe insult in many countries around the world, especially in Muslim countries. Once, a British professor of poetry, while lecturing to a class at an Egyptian university, unintentionally sent a nonverbal message that had disastrous consequences. So carried away was he in talking about a poem that he leaned back in his chair and so revealed the sole of his foot to an astonished class. The Cairo newspaper the next day carried banner headlines about the student demonstration. They **denounced**（谴责）British **arrogance**（自大，傲慢态度）and demanded that the professor be sent home.

Chapter Eight

Intercultural Adaptation, Intercultural Conflict and Intercultural Communication Competence

● **Objectives**

➢ Understand acculturation.
➢ Understand culture shock.
➢ Comprehend the stages of intercultural adaptation.
➢ Understand face and facework.
➢ Acquire some communication styles for managing conflict.
➢ Understand the nature of intercultural communication competence.
➢ Master some strategies for developing intercultural communication competence.

● **导读**

当不同文化群体的人们进行持续不断的直接接触时，一方或双方的原文化类型所产生的变化称为文化适应。任何旅居者从一个国家到另一个国家时都会有一定程度的迷茫、不知所措和情绪波动，这种现象叫做文化休克。文化休克并非是一种精神上的疾病，而是对新环境的一种不适应的反应。文化适应大致可经历五个阶段：蜜月阶段、沮丧阶段、调整阶段、适应阶段和重返母文化阶段。

跨文化冲突，指不同文化成员因在语言、非语言的转换过程中所依据的社会规范的差异而对同一行为、同一现象会做出不同的解释或理解及因此导致的相异、有时甚至是相对立的一种现象。在跨文化交际冲突中，如何维护双方的面子，建构积极身份是一个极为突出的问题。

跨文化交际能力指交际者在具体的环境中商讨文化意蕴、辨析文化身份，有效而得体地进行交际的能力。灵活掌握交际策略可以帮助交际者提高跨文化交际能力，有效而得体地完成交际。

Text

8.1 Intercultural Adaptation

Intercultural adaptation refers broadly to the process of increasing our level of fitness to meet the demands of a new cultural environment (Kim, 1988). It is a long-term process of dealing with **maladjustment** and finally feeling comfortable in the host culture. The transformation process usually involves an intercultural boundary-crossing journey — from security to insecurity, and from familiarity to unfamiliarity. In the journey, identity change is inevitable. The longer the sojourner stays, the more likely his cognitive, **affective**, and behavioral outlook will change.

Intercultural adaptation is a gradual process which cannot occur overnight. The degree of adaptation varies from person to person. Some may adapt well to the host culture pretty soon, while some may find it difficult to face a variety of mismatches. Many factors influence the intercultural adaptation including one's motivation, linguistic competence, education, dual membership, occupational status, uncertainty reduction, mass media usage and communication skills, as well as one's psychological and spiritual strength.

8.1.1 Acculturation

Acculturation refers to an individual's learning and adopting the values and norms of the new host culture while retaining many aspects of his home culture. If a person is highly motivated to be acculturated, he or she usually becomes more culturally involved with group memberships in the host culture than a person who is not motivated to acculturate.

The effects of acculturation can be seen at multiple levels in interacting cultures. At the group level, acculturation often results in changes to culture, customs, and social institutions. Noticeable group level effects of acculturation often include changes in food, clothing, and language. At the individual level, differences in the way individuals acculturate have been shown to be associated not just with changes in daily behavior, but with numerous measures of psychological and physical well-beings.

The ways in which individuals approach acculturation are usually divided into four categories: **assimilation**, **separation**, **integration** and **marginalization**. Assimilation occurs when individuals reject their minority culture and adopt the cultural norms of the dominant or host culture. Separation occurs when individuals reject the host culture in favor of preserving their culture of origin. Separation is often facilitated by immigration to ethnic **enclaves**. Integration occurs when individuals are able to adopt the cultural norms of the host culture while maintaining their culture of origin. Marginalization occurs when individuals reject both their culture of origin and the dominant host culture.

The four categories are used to describe the attitudes of immigrant groups. In fact, they describe the expectations of the larger society of how groups should acculturate. In a melting pot society, in which a harmonious and homogenous culture is promoted, assimilation is the **endorsed** acculturation approach. In segregationist society, in which humans are separated into racial groups in daily life, a separation approach is endorsed. In a multiculturalist society, in which multiple cultures are accepted and appreciated, individuals are encouraged to adopt an integrationist approach to acculturation. In societies where cultural exclusion is promoted,

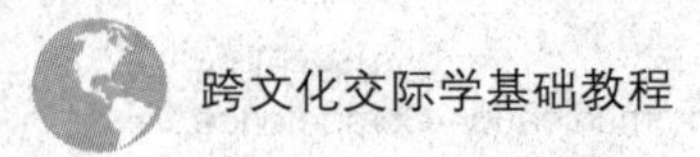

individuals often adopt marginalization approach to acculturation.

Findings of studies conducted in multicultural societies have consistently shown that integration could bring about the most favorable adjustment outcome of immigrants, while marginalization is the most unfavorable, with separation and assimilation in between.

8.1.2 Culture Shock

The phenomenon of culture shock was described in many works of anthropologists in the early 20th century. But it was not until 1960 that the term first appeared in an article of Oberg (1960). Culture shock happens to almost everyone who enters a new culture. It is most noticeable for sojourners to pursue further studies or better career. Probing into culture shock can help us better understand the nature of intercultural adaptation.

8.1.2.1 Nature of Culture Shock

Culture shock refers to the transition period and the accompanying feelings of stress and anxiety a person experiences during the early period upon entering a new culture. It is virtually a communication problem which involves depressed feelings caused by a lack of understanding of the verbal and nonverbal communication of the host culture, its customs, as well as its value systems.

When we are strangers in other cultures, we are confronted with situations in which our mental and behavioral habits are called into question. Such situations produce a conflict in which we are forced to suspend temporarily or abandon our identification with the cultural patterns that have symbolized who we are and what we are. To deal with such **inconsistencies**, most of us are, temporarily at least, in a state of mental and physical disturbance. Many examples of confusion experienced by international students, Peace Corps volunteers, and international business personnel suggest a wide range of responses and reactions to new cultural surroundings. Reactions to such situations have been called culture shock.

It is normal to experience some level of culture shock when many familiar cultural cues and patterns are severed, when our values and beliefs are questioned in a new environment, and when we're continually expected to

perform with appropriate skills and speed before we're able to understand clearly the rules of performance.

8. 1. 2. 2 Symptoms of Culture Shock

Culture shock affects the whole person: body, mind and spirit. Being aware of its symptoms and understanding that it's a natural outcome of an international move are the first step toward overcoming it.

Culture shock involves the following symptoms: sadness, loneliness, homesickness, idealizing the home culture, stereotyping national culture of host, dissatisfaction with life in general, loss of sense of humor, sense of isolation, overwhelming and irrational fears related to the host country, irritability, resentment, family conflict, loss of identity, feelings of inadequacy or insecurity, negative self-image, cognitive fogginess, lack of concentration and depression.

Culture shock is often considered to be primarily a psychosocial condition, and its link to various physical illnesses may be overlooked. Yet it is widely accepted that the mental and emotional exertion necessary to make sense of the new culture has a direct effect on the body's physiological functions. Physiologically speaking, culture shock is precisely this state of weakness, exhaustion, and **susceptibility** to disease.

The physical symptoms of culture shock include: fatigue, **malaise**, generalized aches and pains, increase in illness or accidents, excessive need for sleep or inability to sleep, overeating or lack of appetite, abuse of drugs and/or alcohol.

The physical and psychosocial symptoms of culture shock vary from person to person. For some people, it may take only a few weeks to work through the psychological distress while for some others, it may take quite a long period to overcome the frustration of culture shock. However, acknowledging its existence, and recognizing its many symptoms, will better enable sojourners to implement appropriate strategies for managing culture shock.

8. 1. 2. 3 Effects of Culture Shock

Culture shock can serve both positive and negative implications. The former may conduce to individual growth, while the latter may lead to personal **retrogress**.

In a positive sense, culture shock may contribute to individual growth. First, culture shock provides a learning opportunity that demands new responses from sojourners in tackling a constantly changing environment. Second, culture shock can create an environment and serve as a motivation force for people to move to new levels of self-actualization because most of them have a tendency to pursue unique goals. Third, culture shock can give sojourners a welcome sense of challenge and achievement as a result of dealing with people from rather different backgrounds. Fourth, the consciousness of learning increases when the level of personal anxiety is aroused to a certain degree. Fifth, the experience from culture shock produces new ideas that, in turn, offer people a new set of behavioral responses for future unfamiliar situations.

In a negative sense, culture shock may lead to personal retrogress. First, affectively, culture shock constitutes an unbalancing experience. People might experience the mood of **mania** and excitement. People may feel hysteria, confusion, anxiety, and depression. This uncertainty may be damaging to the psychological growth of some sojourners. Second, cognitively and perceptually, a set of desirable or proper behaviors in one country might be considered bizarre in another country. Sorting through feelings about cultural differences may take a long time. People might encounter the following problems: **psychosomatic** problems such as headaches, stomachaches due to prolonged stress; cognitive disorientation due to difficulties in making accurate attributions; affective upheavals consisting of feelings of loneliness, depression, and drastic mood swings, and awkwardness in social interaction due to the inability to perform optimally in the new language and settings.

8.1.2.4 Strategies for Managing Culture Shock

There are numerous strategies to diminish the severity and manage the symptoms of culture shock.

1) Knowledge-based Strategies for Managing Culture Shock

Many sojourners fail to recognize the symptoms of culture shock, and think there must be something wrong with them. Knowing they're

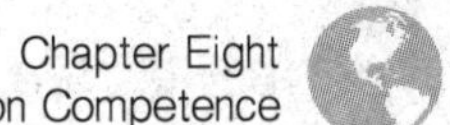

experiencing a normal reaction to an overseas move and not going crazy is a welcome relief and removes a source of anxiety.

Continuing to learn about the host country is a critical step in the battle against culture shock. The more knowledge a sojourner has about the new environment, the better. Observation is a low-risk method of intelligence-gathering that allows the sojourner to learn appropriate behaviors, even if the reasoning behind them isn't yet clear.

Books and websites are good sources of information, but the best resources are natives of the new country. Most people are proud of their culture, and delighted in showing it off to newcomers. Asking questions with genuine curiosity often leads to a wealth of information. Cross-cultural training, either pre-departure or in-country, is another useful option.

Making friends with local people is rewarding on many levels. It's especially helpful if the person is willing to act as a cultural informant. Making connections within the host community is also beneficial, as it reduces feelings of alienation and loneliness. However, sojourners should guard against using **compatriots** as an excuse to isolate themselves from the host culture.

2) Emotion-based Strategies for Managing Culture Shock

The most effective approach to managing culture shock involves an attitude adjustment on the part of the sojourner. Keeping an open mind is critical. The sojourner who views the new culture with an attitude of openness and respect will have a far better outcome than one who is suspicious and critical.

Tips to limit the effects of culture shock are:

To adjust one's attitude by viewing the time overseas as an opportunity for personal growth.

To break out of one's comfort zone, even if it's just for a few minutes each day to start.

To record one's experiences, thoughts, and feelings in a journal.

To have a sense of humor, and faith in one's abilities.

To socialize with local people.

To make the effort to learn and use the language.

To nurture family relationships.

To set small, achievable goals and regularly evaluate their progress.

3) Physical Strategies for Managing Culture Shock

The stresses associated with sojourners' life invariably cause physical tension, which can lead to illness if not relieved.

Good physical habits are vitally important in the battle against culture shock. Daily physical activity is recommended, along with some form of relaxation therapy such as **yoga**, meditation, or **massage**. Other effective strategies include getting adequate sleep and fresh air, eating balanced meals, and limiting alcohol intake.

Avoiding culture shock entirely may not be possible. In fact, experiencing culture shock may be a necessary step on the journey to cultural adjustment. Fortunately, its weak effects can be managed with the right strategies.

8.1.3 Stages of Intercultural Adaptation

Over the past decades, many scholars of sojourner adaptation have been studying the short-term adaptive changes that follow the initial phase of culture shock.

The most popular pattern of intercultural adaptation is known as "U-curve" pattern based on Lysgaard's (1955) study on 200 Norwegian Fulbright scholars in the United States. The curve describes the initial optimism and excitement in the host culture, the subsequent dip in the level of adaptation, and the following gradual recovery. It predicts the psychological change in sojourners. Gullahorn & Gullahorn (1963) further develops the pattern and the "U-curve" has been extended to the "W-curve" with the addition of a reentry phase of the sojourn experience.

Generally speaking, the W-curve pattern comprises five stages: honeymoon period, crisis period, adjustment period, biculturalism period, and reentry period.

Honeymoon Period

The honeymoon stage is the initial period of the intercultural adaptation. This stage is characterized by fascination with the new culture and by the excitement about all the new things people encounter in the host culture. In

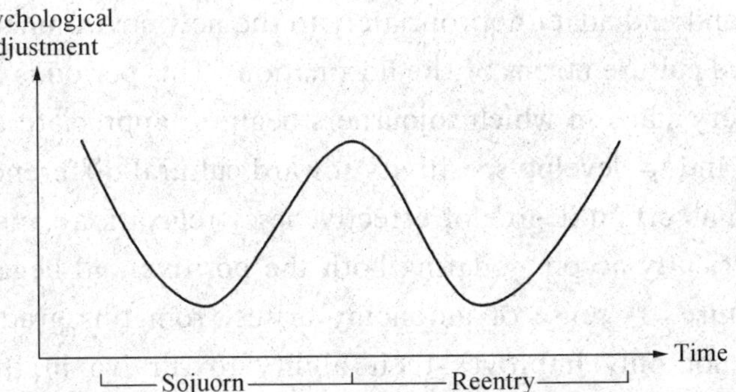

Figure 8.1 The U-curve and W-curve adaptive change of sojourners

Adapted from Intercultural Communication: A Reader by Larry A. Samovar & Richard E. Porter, 2000.

this stage, people are still viewing the new environment from the host culture perspective. Their curiosity in this stage often provides them with a feeling of excitement when they detect similarities and differences between the original and the new cultures.

Crisis Period

The crisis period is also called the hostility or frustration stage. Sojourners in this stage must directly face the challenges of the new culture on a day-to-day basis. This stage is characterized by frequent confusion and disintegration as they confront differences in values, beliefs, behaviors, and lifestyles. Activities that they take for granted suddenly become insurmountable problems. Such problems often lead to a feeling of rejecting or being rejected by the host culture. The increasing sense of being different, isolated, and inadequate to the demands of the host culture also leads sojourners to assert the superiority of their own culture. The symptoms of being too **ethnocentric** tend to challenge the sojourners' personality and to confuse their identity. If the sojourners are unable to overcome these problems, severe depression and withdrawal will ruin their life in the new environment.

Adjustment Period

Efforts to cope with the problems in the crisis period gradually provide sojourners with new ways to live in the new culture. Sojourners begin to learn how to respond and adapt appropriately to the new environment by following the social and culture norms of the host nation. This period is also referred to as the recovery stage in which sojourners begin to appreciate and respect the new culture and to develop sensitivity toward cultural differences. Sojourners might regain a certain degree of effectiveness, relaxation, and comfort, and have less difficulty accommodating both the positive and negative aspects of the host culture. A sense of autonomy arises from this gradual adjustment period that not only improves their ability to survive in the new culture without the assistance of cultural cues from the home culture but also marks a growth in their personal flexibility.

Biculturalism Period

In biculturalism, or the mastery period, people may still experience occasional anxiety and frustration, but they have cultivated an understanding of the host culture and can begin to work and play in the new environment with a feeling of enjoyment. They recover or nearly recover from the symptoms of culture shock. This stage is marked by attitudes and behaviors that are independent from the influence of their birth. It is this fully developed autonomy that provides them with the freedom and capacity for dual cultural identity, awareness of being in control of creative enjoyment, aesthetic appreciation for the contrasts of cultures, development of satisfactory interpersonal relationships, and a high level of commitment toward both cultural contexts.

Reentry Period

Reentry is the process that an individual goes through when returning to the home culture after a sojourn. Returning home is often more difficult than going overseas, partly because reentry shock is usually a surprise to the individual, who does not expect to have adjustment problems in going home. These unfulfilled expectations are due to faulty memory, to selective recall, and to the fact that the home culture has already changed in noticeable ways while the sojourner is gone for several months or a couple of years. The sojourner's expectations do not fit the reality, and he or she again becomes depressed. This reentry period may last for several months before the sojourner once again feels at home. Finally the sojourner will find that the

price he or she has paid for his or her overseas sojourn is the bargain of a lifetime.

8.2 Intercultural Conflict

Conflict is inevitable in all social and personal relationships. It exists whenever incompatible activities occur. Conflicts can range from minor disagreements, such as differences in opinion with individuals with whom we have ongoing relationships, to wars. Understanding the nature of conflict and how our cultures and ethnicities influence our approaches to conflict is critical to developing and maintaining relationships with others in interaction.

8.2.1 Nature of Conflict

In the context of intercultural encounters, conflict is defined as the perceived or actual incompatibility of values, expectations, processes, or outcomes between two or more parties from different cultures over relational issues. Such differences are often expressed through different cultural conflict styles. Intercultural conflict typically starts off with miscommunication. Miscommunication often leads to misinterpretation. If the miscommunication goes unmanaged, it can become an actual interpersonal conflict.

Conflict in relationships can be overt and out in the open or can be out of sight. When conflict is out of sight, it is easy to avoid addressing it. In fact, avoidance is probably the most widely used strategy for dealing with conflict. One reason we avoid conflict is that many of us view conflict negatively. Conflict itself, however, is not positive or negative. How we manage the conflicts we have can produce positive or negative consequences toward our relationships with others.

8.2.2 Face

Face is a concept that is concerned with people's sense of worth, dignity and identity and is associated with issues such as respect, honor, status, reputation and competence. Face is a universal phenomenon: everyone has the same basic face concerns. However, culture can affect the relative sensitivity of different aspects of people's face, as well as which strategies are most appropriate for managing face.

There are three types of face: self-face, other-face, and mutual-face. Self-face is the concern for one's own image; other-face is the concern for another's image, and mutual-face is the concern for both parties' images or the image of the relationship. Face emerges in the flow of events in our interactions with others. We defend our self-face and protect other-face during interactions.

Concern about one's face or dignity is universal. What is different from culture to culture is the personal characteristics on which one's dignity depends and the social priority given to preserving one's own dignity, the dignity of others, and the dignity of important groups to which the person belongs. Face can be lost, saved, and given. It can also be threatened, enhanced, undermined and bargained over both emotionally and cognitively. Generally, persons of individualistic cultures have a greater concern for self-face and less concern for other-face than members of collectivistic cultures.

8.2.3 Facework

Facework refers to the strategies used to threaten or support others' face and protect self-face when conflicts are managed. The way individuals manage their face varies across cultures. Chinese tend to use avoiding, obliging facework tactics; Germans and U.S. Americans do not avoid conflict and use direct, confrontational facework tactics (e.g. problem-solving); Japanese and Mexicans prefer to use facework tactics that allow them to avoid direct confrontation. It is generally concluded that emphasizing independent self-construal is associated with defending and remaining calm facework tactics, and emphasizing interdependent self-construal is associated with problem-solving, respect, apologizing, pretending, private discussion, and giving in facework tactics.

Facework tactics are often linked with face-concern. Generally speaking, self-face concerns are associated with aggressive and defensive facework tactics; other-face concerns are associated with giving in, avoiding, pretending, and third-party facework tactics; and mutual-face concerns are

associated with problem-solving, private discussion, apologizing, and compromising facework tactics.

8.2.4 Cultural Differences in Managing Conflict

Culture influences the way people think about conflicts and their preferences for managing them.

Members of individualistic cultures often separate the issues on which they have conflicts from the people with whom they have conflicts. Members of collectivistic cultures, in contrast, generally do not make this distinction. Japanese managers may take criticism and objections to ideas they express as personal attacks. U.S. American managers, however, do not take criticism of their ideas as personal attacks unless they are highly defensive.

Members of individualistic cultures are likely to possess a confrontational, direct attitude toward conflicts while members of collectivistic cultures are likely to possess a non-confrontational, indirect attitude toward conflicts. A direct approach to conflict in individualistic cultures probably stems from the "doing" orientation and the use of linear logic. Members of collectivistic cultures have a strong desire for ingroup harmony and tend to use indirect forms of communication to maintain harmony and, therefore, tend to prefer non-confrontational approaches to conflict.

Members of individualistic cultures take a short-term view of managing conflicts while members of collectivistic cultures take a long-term view of managing conflicts. Members of individualistic cultures are concerned with the immediate conflict situations. Members of collectivistic cultures, in contrast, focus on long-term relationships with others. The immediate conflict is important, but the critical issue for collectivists is whether they can depend on others over the long term.

Members of collectivistic cultures prefer to use **mediators** to manage conflicts more than members of individualistic cultures. The use of mediators allows conflicts to be managed without direct confrontation. If confrontation can be avoided, harmony in the relationship can be maintained. Members of individualistic cultures also use mediators to manage conflicts, but they prefer formal mediators (e.g. lawyers) more than members of collectivistic cultures.

In handling disagreements, individualists rely on their own experiences and training while collectivists rely on formal rules and procedures. Collectivists have a greater desire to maintain self-other bonds and are more concerned with others' evaluations of them than individualists.

8.3 Intercultural Communication Competence

Although the study of intercultural communication can be dated back to the works of political scientists and anthropologists in the 1940s and 1950s, the topic of intercultural communication competence remains a fresh area. Intercultural communication competence is the only means whereby we can move beyond cultural differences in order to succeed in intercultural interactions.

8.3.1 Nature of Intercultural Communication Competence

Intercultural communication competence is the degree to which an individual is able to exchange information effectively and appropriately with individuals who belong to a different culture. Intercultural communication competence can be defined as the ability to negotiate cultural meanings and to appropriately execute effective communication behaviors that recognize each other's multiple identities in a specific environment (Guo-ming Chen & William J. Starosta, 1996).

In addition to looking at communication competence as effective and appropriate interaction, intercultural communication scholars place more emphasis on contextual factors. They conceive communication competence not only as effective and appropriate interaction between people but as an effective and appropriate interaction between people who belong to particular environments. Competent persons should not only know how to interact effectively and appropriately with people and environment, but also know how to fulfill their own communication goals by respecting and affirming the multi-level cultural identities of the interactants.

8.3.2 Strategies for Improving Intercultural Communication Competence

How can you perform better in intercultural contexts? The following strategies may help you develop skills in intercultural interactions.

Reduction in ethnocentrism. The destructive effects of judgmental attitudes and a feeling of being superior to others from another cultural group are well documented. Prejudice and ethnocentrism are difficult barriers and often block adequate cultural adjustment and relationship formation in the host culture. Even in the middle of the down stage of culture shock, it is important to keep your criticism of the culture and negative attitudes toward host country foreigners to a minimum. Your intercultural counterparts will appreciate your attempts at being understanding rather than critical.

Tolerance for ambiguity. Tolerance for ambiguity implies the ability to deal successfully with situations even when a lot of information needed to interact effectively is unknown. The ability to react to new but ambiguous situations with little difficulty is a significant skill in intercultural communication. If we have a high tolerance for ambiguity, we tend to seek objective information about the situation and the strangers in it. Further, we tend to be open to new information about ourselves and others if we have a high tolerance for ambiguity. Lack of tolerance for ambiguity involves perceiving ambiguous situations as threatening and undesirable. The greater our tolerance for ambiguity, the more comfortable we feel in situations where we do not have all the information we would like.

Empathetic communication. To understand things from another's point of view is critical in a number of circumstances, including communicating innovative ideas and performing up to our potential in intercultural communication. **Empathy** involves ① carefully listening to others, ② understanding others' feelings, ③ being interested in what others say, ④ being sensitive to others' needs, and ⑤ understanding others' points of view. Empathy can be increased if you resist the tendency to interpret the other's verbal and nonverbal actions from your culture's orientation.

Communication openness. To be open in intercultural communication, people should first work to emphasize areas of similarity with others. To the extent they can understand commonality, generally the better the interpersonal relationship. Then they should try to accept differing opinions. Recognizing differences often facilitates effective communication. Once individuals satisfy their curiosity about differences, understanding can occur.

Self-esteem and confidence. Self-esteem predicts intercultural effectiveness. Self-confidence also correlates with personal adjustment and performance. Fear can freeze one's emotions and spirits. At the root of some fear is low self-esteem. Beyond those momentary losses of confidence, however, most of us can really perform beyond our expectations.

Avoidance of self-centered communication. Self-centered communication is less effective in intercultural contexts. Examples include calling attention to oneself, bragging, and showing disinterest in the ideas of the group. In Japan, making excuses for why something did not work out does not work as well as a simple apology. In general, excessive self-praise or self-blame usually are ineffective in intercultural interactions.

Innovativeness. Innovativeness refers to one's ability to try new things, to engage in some social risk taking, particular where new information and developing social relationships are concerned. Evidence suggests that the ability to try new things is linked with intercultural effectiveness. A willingness to experiment with new approaches and especially a willingness to learn are highly linked with intercultural success.

Conversation management. This area refers to social skills such as interpersonal harmony, responsiveness in conversation, self-monitoring and self-disclosure appropriate to the culture. These imply turn-taking and the ability to adapt interaction goals and behaviors to others. Also keeping cultural rules and practicing etiquette are conversational skills. Some individuals are skilled at starting and ending interactions among interactants and at taking turns and maintaining communication. These conversation management skills are important because through them all interactants in an interaction are able to speak and contribute appropriately. In contrast, dominating conversations or being **submissive** in conversations is harmful to intercultural effectiveness. Listening to others, inviting their explanations, and showing genuine interest are communication suggestions. Although

domination can prove to be harmful, if you are overly submissive, others may decide you have nothing to contribute, which leads to the disappearance of intercultural relationship. Continuing to engage people in conversations long after they have begun to display signs of disinterest and boredom or ending conversations abruptly may also pose problems. Conversation management also requires knowing how to indicate turn taking both verbally and nonverbally.

Management of communication anxiety. The higher the communication apprehension, the lower the intercultural effectiveness. To manage our anxiety, the most important thing we can do is to break away from the situation in which we feel anxious. This might mean excusing ourselves to leave the room or mentally withdraw for a short period of time. We need to calm ourselves and allow our anxious feelings to pass and then return to the situation. To restore our calm, we can use various techniques to control the physical symptoms associated with our anxiety. These may include yoga, **hypnotism**, meditation, and progressive muscular relaxation.

Interpersonal comfort. Research also shows that our ability to feel comfortable interpersonally is significantly correlated with maximum intercultural adjustment. Other research indicates that interpersonal trust, interpersonal interest, interpersonal harmony and interaction are correlated with intercultural effectiveness. Thus, if you do not feel comfortable with your interpersonal relationships in your home culture, you may not feel any more comfortable in a host culture.

To sum up, as the world population grows more aware of its interdependence, it confronts ever shifting cultural, ecological, economic, and technological realities that define the shrinking world of the 21st century. To develop newer ways of living in the world together, to see things through the eyes of others, and to add the knowledge of others to our personal repertoire become crucial for further human progress. This global mindset can only result from competent intercommunication among peoples from diverse cultures. Only with mastery of intercultural communication competence can persons from different cultures communicate effectively and appropriately in the upcoming global society.

New Words and Phrases

maladjustment /ˌmæləˈdʒʌstmənt/ *n*. 失调,不适应
affective /əˈfektɪv/ *adj*. 情感的,表达感情的
enclave /ˈenkleɪv/ *n*. 飞地(指在本国境内的隶属另一国的一块领土)
endorse /ɪnˈdɔːs/ *vt*. (公开地)赞同,认可
inconsistency /ɪnkənˈsɪst(ə)nsi/ *n*. 不一致,不协调
susceptibility /səˌseptəˈbɪlɪti/ *n*. 易受影响,敏感性
malaise /mæˈleɪz/ *n*. 不适,心神不安
retrogress /ˌretrəˈgres/ *n*. 倒退,退化
mania /ˈmeɪnjə/ *n*. 狂热,狂躁
psychosomatic /ˌsaɪkəʊsəʊˈmætɪk/ *adj*. 身心的,身心失调的
compatriot /kəmˈpætrɪət/ *n*. 同国人,同胞
yoga /ˈjəʊgə/ *n*. 瑜伽,瑜伽术
massage /ˈmæsɑːʒ/ *n*. 按摩
ethnocentric /ˌeθnəʊˈsentrɪk/ *adj*. 种族优越感的,民族中心主义的
mediator /ˈmiːdɪeɪtə/ *n*. 调停者,调解者
submissive /səbˈmɪsɪv/ *adj*. 顺从的,唯命是从的
hypnotism /ˈhɪpnətɪz(ə)m/ *n*. 催眠术
acculturation 涵化
assimilation 同化
separation 分离
integration 整合
marginalization 边缘化
culture shock 文化休克,文化震荡
self-construal 自我理解
ethnocentrism 民族优越感
intercultural communication competence 跨文化交际能力
empathy 移情

Exercises

I. Questions for discussion

1. How does culture shock influence us both physically and spiritually?

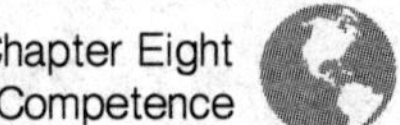

2. How does reentry shock occur? What should we do to manage the shock?
3. How do you understand the concept of face?
4. How does culture influence our preference for conflict style?
5. How should we understand the effectiveness and appropriateness of intercultural communication competence?

II. Multiple choice

Directions: Choose the best answer to each of the following questions.

1. Which approach to acculturation is adopted when individuals are able to adopt the cultural norms of the dominant or host culture while maintaining their culture of origin?
   A. Assimilation B. Separation
   C. Integration D. Marginalization
2. Which is **Not** the physical symptom of culture shock?
   A. Lack of appetite B. Sense of isolation
   C. Abuse of drugs D. Susceptibility to disease
3. In which stage of intercultural adaptation have sojourners recovered or nearly recovered from the symptoms of culture shock and begun to work and play in the host culture with a feeling of enjoyment?
   A. honeymoon period B. crisis period
   C. adjustment period D. biculturalism period
4. Which type of face concerns are associated with problem-solving, private discussion, apologizing and compromising facework tactics?
   A. Self-face B. Other-face
   C. Mutual-face D. Group face
5. If you are skilled at carefully listening to others, understanding others' feelings, and being sensitive to others' needs, it means that you are ________.
   A. highly empathetic B. highly tolerant
   C. highly ethnocentric D. highly open minded

III. Comprehension check

Directions: Decide whether the following statements are true (T) or false (F).

________ 1. The more highly motivated to be acculturated an individual is, the more likely he or she is to be culturally involved with group membership.

________2. In a melting pot society, individuals are encouraged to adopt integration as an approach to acculturation.

________3. If a sojourner experiences culture shock, there must be something wrong with him or her.

________4. In the honeymoon stage of intercultural adaptation, sojourners tend to neglect differences and reinforce the similarities between the host culture and their own culture.

________5. Avoidance is probably the most widely used strategy for dealing with conflict because conflict itself is negative.

________6. Japanese managers may view others' criticism of their ideas as personal attacks.

________7. In intercultural encounters, the use of mediators can help manage conflicts without direct confrontation.

________8. As a negative conflict style, avoidance cannot help to maintain face harmony and mutual face dignity.

Case Study

Case I

Nguyen Chau Van Loc went to the United States in 1979 from Vietnam. His first impression of the U.S. was very positive. He felt that this new environment offered him many exciting opportunities.

However, Loc quickly found himself unprepared to take advantage of these opportunities. He knew almost no English. Even when he knew what to say on a bus or in a store, no one understood him, and he had to repeat and repeat. In Vietnam, Loc was a technician, but in the U.S., he didn't have enough experience compared with others. He had trouble finding a job. He felt that he did not have important role or position in the city and missed the security and friendliness of his town in Vietnam. He felt that he would never learn English or feel happy in the U.S. He began to feel very depressed and homesick.

With the help of a counselor in his English program, he understood that his feelings were normal and that they were only a stage in his adjustment to the new culture. He learned that many other Vietnamese felt the same way as he did. Some, in fact, were more disoriented than he was and were afraid to go out into the city.

Eventually, Loc began to feel better about his life in the U.S. He developed a position in the Vietnamese American community and adjusted to his new role in the American society. He is accustomed to his life in the new country but will always miss Vietnam.

Questions for Discussion

1. What is Loc's first impression of the U.S. when he went to the United States?
2. What has made Loc feel depressed and homesick?
3. How do you understand culture shock from Loc's experience in America?

Case Analysis

Culture shock occurs as a result of total immersion in a new culture, as Loc's story manifests. From his experience in the United States, we see there are, generally speaking, three stages of culture shock. In the first stage, the newcomers are fascinated with the new things they encounter in the new culture and like the new environment. Then, when the newness wears off and problems arise, they begin to dislike or feel disappointed with things in the new culture. In the final stage, the newcomers begin to adjust to their surroundings and, as a result, enjoy their life more.

As the case shows, Loc's first impression of America was very positive and he was quite excited about the new surroundings. He was experiencing the honeymoon stage of culture shock. But soon he found himself unable to communicate with others and even hard to find a job, because he knew no English and had no enough working experience as a technician. Then with a sense of loss and isolation, he began to feel depressed and homesick, which are typical symptoms of the second stage of culture shock. When he finally realized that his feelings were normal and tried to adjust to the new culture, he began to feel better. In this stage, culture shock is disappearing.

Case II

Kevin, who grew up in Madison, Wisconsin, is a student at the University of Wisconsin. Kevin is enrolled in an introductory communication course. The professor has assigned Kevin and Kokkeong, an international exchange student from Malaysia, to work on a project together. The professor has given them the option of either submitting a paper or giving a presentation. Kevin and Kokkeong disagree on which option to pursue. Kevin prefers the presentation option, while Kokkeong prefers the paper option. The following conversation ensues.

Kevin: Well, Kokkeong, I think we should do a presentation. I hate writing papers.

Kokkeong: Well, what have other students done?

Kevin: Who cares?

Kokkeong: Well, maybe they might have some advice.

Kevin: Advice about what?

Kokkeong: About which assignment is preferred.

Kevin: Look, I already know what assignment I prefer.

Kokkeong: I wonder if we should ask the professor for his advice.

Kevin: Why? He's already given us the option. Look, I've been a student here for two years. I know how these things work. Let's just do the presentation.

Kokkeong: I think I'll ask some others what they think.

Kevin: Go ahead and do what you want, but I'm not budging. We're doing a presentation. I know what I'm talking about.

Questions for Discussion

1. How does the conflict between Kevin and Kokkeong arise?
2. How does Kevin deal with the conflict and what conflict style does he adopt?
3. How does Kokkeong deal with the conflict and what conflict style does he adopt?

Case Analysis

In the case, Kevin was born and raised in the United States, a typical individualistic, low-context culture. Americans are expected to take the

initiative in advancing their personal interests and well-beings and to be direct and assertive in interacting with others. In the conversation, Kevin asserts forcefully. He stresses his own experience and expertise on the matter of presentations versus papers. His approach is typical of a dominating conflict style.

Kokkeong grew up in Malaysia, a collectivistic, high-context culture. In the culture, people lay emphasis on the views, needs and goals of the group rather than oneself. Ingroup harmony is more important. Therefore, they tend to communicate in an indirect fashion. In the conversation, Kokkeong tries to convince Kevin that they should seek the advice of some third party, either other students or the professor. His approach is typical of a non-confrontational conflict style.

Further Reading

Reading I

The Chinese Concept of Face

Chinese tend to be obsessed with face as a sacred object to be seen by the community. This sacred object (face) is for the community, of the community, by the community, and in the community. It is a communal object nurtured and protected by all through community-oriented feelings, action, and being. Physically, everyone has a distinct face, but the face as the sacred object should be shared and guarded by all. Every physical face is but a constituent of this sacred dynamic. If one is not capable of protecting one's own face, one is violating this communal code. This represents a special kind of personhood — the ideal Chinese personhood with each person preferably enmeshed with other persons and each family as an inseparable member of the empire/nation. The rationale for treating the face as the sacred object seems to be like this:

Face holds the uppermost and frontal position in the body. Self, to the Chinese, resides in the chest, below the face, something of a lower level and primarily remains "asleep"; hips are treated as if they were not part of the body. A story goes that in the military coup called the Xi'an Incident in 1937, the Chinese Nationalist Government Leader Chiang Kai-shek hid himself in a small and shallow cave in the Li Hill near Xi'an City, China, with his hands covering his face inside the cave, and with his hips and legs protruding outside it. This act suggests that he, like an average Chinese, was more concerned with saving his own face (here by covering it) than saving his own life. As a result, he was still caught by one of his rebellious inferiors. If you were to pat or even slap a Chinese person on the hips, he or she would feel that you are being playful with him or her. The feet occupy the lowest part of the body. To ask a Chinese person to walk on the head with the feet upwards or to ask him or her to cross between someone else's legs are some of the traditional Chinese interpersonal strategies to cause him or her to lose face. For example, someone who is not able to pay a debt may be forced by the lender to do so while calling the lender "grandpa" or "grandma". Then, the lender would release the person from the debt because he had gained a lot of face by having had the other person crawling across his legs and call him "ancestor". By walking on the victim's own head and by crossing between the victimizer's legs, the victim's face is positioned at the same height as the victimizer's hips. Natural hierarchies inspire the Chinese notion of social hierarchy. Therefore, it is the Chinese logic that the human body is a structure of physical hierarchy in which the face is positioned at the highest level and thus treated as a sacred object and symbol instead of any other parts of the body below the face that are closer to the ground.

Traditionally, Chinese tend to have few indigenous gods, and the few gods they have play only a marginal role in organizing social activities. Instead, the Chinese have a strong tradition of ancestor worship. This ancestor worship is carried out through daily observance of the face. It is a typical Chinese belief that either dead ancestors wish that their offsprings will glorify them (earn them face) or that the living members of the clan or community will see to it that their descendants live up to the dead ancestors' expectations. Someone who fails is said to have besmeared his or her dead ancestors' faces, or to have caused them to lose face in heaven. In this sense, one's own identity is intimately linked to one's dead ancestors' identity.

Internal or ritualistic communication with one's dead ancestors functions to motivate one to fulfill communal expectations.

Finally but perhaps most importantly, face practices are the enactment of the real Chinese personhood — *junzi*, meaning "gentleman". Confucius classifies people into two kinds — *junzi* and *xiao ren* (mean persons). A *junzi* is said to have *mianzi*, which is maintained by a higher social status or position and commands a higher level of respect from the community, along with wider access to both symbolic and material resources. A *xiao ren* is one without any status or position, thus with neither *mianzi* nor *lian* — the lowest level of humanity as determined by social conduct demonstrating low moral character. Confucius uses the same words for "gentleman" and "emperor", suggesting that all people should emulate their Emperor as the moral model. Those who have done so successfully are called *junzi*. According to the ideal, a *junzi* should be like an Emperor who is able to maintain harmony throughout society as well as in his social and family relations through appealing to human feelings and cultivating virtues such as *ren* (benevolence), *yi* (righteousness), *li* (rites), *zhi* (aspiration), and *xeng* (trust). This junzihood is achieved through expanding *mianzi* until it embraces the whole community and ideally all of humanity.

To conclude, the Chinese concept of face reflects a unique Chinese view of what a person should be and how this type of personhood can be constructed through the hierarchically structured, communally oriented, relationally and morally defined, emotionally anchored, and harmony-driven face negotiation. One's life may be over with the death of the body, but his or her face remains a part of the community.

Adapted from Intercultural Communication: A Reader by Larry A. Samovar & Richard E. Porter, 2000.

Reading II

Levels of Intercultural Awareness

Intercultural awareness is a process which can be integrated into three

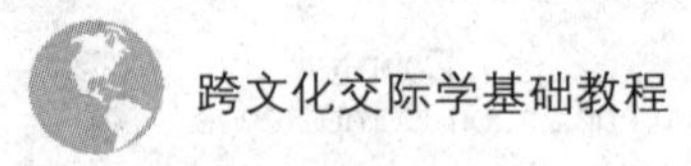

levels: ① awareness of superficial cultural traits, ② awareness of significant and subtle cultural traits that contrast markedly with another's, and ③ awareness of how another culture feels from the insider's perspective.

The first level is the understanding of another culture based mainly on stereotypes. The awareness in this level tends to be superficial and often partial. Information about the culture comes from the media, tourism books, textbooks, or the first impression. For example, U. S. Americans are perceived as outgoing, friendly, loud, hard working, wasteful, wealthy people by foreigners. In this level, one tends to understand a culture or its people by the most visible characteristics it possesses. Then some of these characteristics are applied to the whole group. For example, Asian students with a high GPA in American colleges are often incorrectly considered as science and math majors because the media reports that Asian students often do better in those areas. Finally, the same treatment is given to each member of the group by saying, for example, "You are Japanese, you must be smart."

The second level of intercultural awareness shows how significant and subtle cultural traits differ sharply form one's own through direct or secondhand experience. This level has two phases. The first phase approaches intercultural awareness through culture-conflict situations and the second through intellectual analysis. Although the media, tourism books or textbooks may provide contrasting information, one does not fully feel or grasp the real meaning of the cultural differences except through experience by direct or indirect interactions with people of another culture. In the first phase of this level, the experience of cultural conflict may lead to depression, helplessness, hostility, anxiety, withdrawal, or disorientation, but at the same time it provides the chance to further recognize and understand another's culture. The feeling in this phase resembles culture shock in the process of intercultural adjustment.

Many sojourners, such as Peace Corps volunteers and foreign students, experience stress during this phase of intercultural awareness. If they are unable to overcome the symptoms of culture shock, then development of intercultural awareness will be halted in this frustrating stage, and culture-

conflict situations will continue to exist in which they feel alienated and marginalized. At this point, the conflict situations that lead to culture shock may impede the process of being aware of the host culture.

In the second phase of the second level of intercultural awareness, through rational and intellectual analysis, one comes to understand that cultural differences can be justified from the other culture's perspective. In other words, differences in cultural traits begin to make sense. Differences then become believable and acceptable. This believability through understanding helps sojourners fully adjust to the host culture. In this phase sojourners begin to appreciate and respect the new culture and to develop sensitivity toward cultural differences. Cultural differences in this phase are processed with a positive effect. This provides motivational force to move one forward to a higher level of intercultural awareness. In addition, intercultural understanding in this phase results from drawing comparisons and contrasts. This practice promotes the learning of cultures that have not yet been experienced.

Finally, the third level of intercultural awareness requires the ability to see the culture from an insider's perspective through empathy. The believability through understanding explicated in phase two of the second level is enhanced by intellectual analysis and by subjective familiarity. In other words, one needs to foster the power of flexibility to make psychic shifts. The power of flexibility is nourished by empathy. Empathy helps one to estimate what is inside another's mind and to share their experience. This selfless and affectively sensitive process helps one to more accurately estimate behaviors or internal states of mind in counterparts that are different from one's own.

Empathy is the ability to project feelings to others with a shared epistemology. This parallels the stage of duality or biculturalism in the intercultural adjustment process through which the fully developed autonomy provides us with the freedom and ability to approach dual cultural identity, awareness of being in control of creative enjoyment, aesthetic appreciation for the contrasts of cultures, development of satisfactory interpersonal relationships, and a high level of commitment toward both cultural contexts.

The developmental levels show that intercultural awareness is a learning process by which one becomes aware of his or her own cognitive growth, learning, and change regarding a set of cultural situations and cultural principles stemming from intercultural communication. It is a part of cognitive function regarding the knowing of how people's outlook, attitudes, values, and behavior are based on cultural dispositions. Thus, intercultural awareness involves change and movement from one cultural frame of reference to another and provides unlimited opportunity for contrast and comparison resulting from cultural differences. A clearer picture of cultural maps, cultural themes, or cultural grammars emerges through this process.

Adapted from intercultural Communication: A Reader by Larry A. Samovar & Richard E. Porter, 2000.

References

[1] ADLER P. S. The transitional experience: An alternative view of culture shock [J]. Journal of Humanistic Psychology, 1975,15:13 - 23.

[2] ALTMAN I. Privacy Regulation: Culturally Universal or Culturally Specific? [J]. Journal of Social Issues, 1977,83(3):66 - 84.

[3] ANDERSEN P. A. Consciousness, cognition, and communication [J]. Western Journal of Speech Communication, 1986,50:87 - 101.

[4] ANDERSEN P, LUSTIG M, & ANDERSEN J. Changes in latitude, changes in attitude [J]. Communication Quarterly, 1990,38:291 - 311.

[5] ARGYLE M. Bodily communication [M]. New York: International Universities Press, 1975.

[6] BARNLUND D. Interpersonal communication [M]. Boston: Houghton Mifflin, 1968.

[7] BECKER C. B. Reasons for the lack of argumentation and debate in the Far East [J]. International Journal of Intercultural Relations, 1986,10:75 - 92.

[8] BERRY J. W, SAM D T. Acculturation and Adaptation. //J W BERRY, M H SEGALL, C KAGITCIBASA (Eds.). Handbook of Cross-Cultural Psychology: Social Behavior and Applications (1997, Vol. 3, pp. 291 - 326). Boston: Allyn & Bacon.

[9] BIRDWHISTELL R L. Introduction to Kinesics [M]. Philadelphia: University of Pennsylvania Press. 1970:318 - 319.

[10] BIRDWHISTELL R. Kinesics in context [M]. Philadelphia: University of Pennsylvania Press, 1970.

[11] BOWERS J W, BRADAC J J. Issues in Communication Theory: A Metatheoretical Analysis. //M BURGOON (Ed.). Communication Yearbook 5 (1982: 3). New Brunswick, NJ: Transaction Books.

[12] BROWN P, LEVINSON S. Universals in Language usage. //E. Goody (Ed.),

Questions and politeness. Cambridge, UK: Cambridge University Press, 1978.

[13] BURGOON J K. Nonverbal communication: The unspoken dialogue [M]. New York: Harper & Row, 1978.

[14] EDWARDS J. Language, society, and identity [M]. Oxford, UK: Blackwell, 1985.

[15] CARLEY H DODD. Dynamics of intercultural communication [M]. Shanghai: Shanghai Foreign Language Education Press, 2006.

[16] CHARLES DARWIN. Expression of the Emotions in Man and Animals. London, John Murray/University of Chicago Press, 1872.

[17] CHEN G M. Intercultural communication competence: Some perspectives of research [M]. The Howard Journal of Communication, 1990,2:243 - 261.

[18] CHEN G M, STAROSTA W J. Intercultural communication competence: A synthesis. //B BURLESON (Ed.), Communication yearbook 19, 1996. Thousand Oaks, CA: Sage.

[19] CHEN G M, STAROSTA W J. Foundations of Intercultural Communication. Boston: Allyn & Bacon, 1998.

[20] CHOMSKY N. Syntactic Structures [M]. The Hague: Mouth & Company, 1957.

[21] CHOMSKY N. Aspects of the Theory of Syntax. Cambridge: MIT Press, 1965; Goss, B. & O'Hair, D. Communicating in Interpersonal Relationships. New York: Macmillan, 1988.

[22] CONDON J C, Yousef F. An Introduction to Intercultural Communication [M]. Indianapolis, IN: Bobbs-Merrill, 1975.

[23] DANCE F E X. The Function of Human Communication: A Theoretical Approach [M]. New York: Hold, Rinehart and Winston, 1976.

[24] EDWARD SAPIR. Language: An Introduction to the Study of Speech [M]. New York: Harcourt Brace, 1921.

[25] FARB P. Word Play: What Happens When People Talk [M]. New York: Bantam, 1973:234.

[26] FISHER B A. Interpersonal Communication: Pragmatics of Human Relationships [M]. New York: Random House, 1994:22.

[27] FROMKIN V, RODMAN R. An Introduction to Language (5th ed.) [M]. New York: Holt, Rinehart and Winston, 1993

[28] FURNHAM A, BOCHNER S. Culture shock: Psychological reactions to unfamiliar environments [M]. London: Methuen, 1986.

[29] FURNHAM A. The adjustment of sojourners [M]. //KIM, GUDYKUNST WB, Editors. Cross-Cultural Adaptation: Current Approaches. Newbury Park, CA: Sage Publications, 1988:36 - 52.

[30] GOODMAN, N. R. Cross-Cultural Training for the Global Executive [M]. //R W BRISLIN, T YOSHIDA (Eds.). Improving Intercultural Interaction: Models for Cross-Cultural Training Programs (1994:34 - 54). Thousand Oaks, CA: Sage.

[31] GOSS B. Communication in Everyday Life. Belmont, CA: Wadsworth, Gudykunst (Eds.), Cross-cultural adaptation. Newbury Park, CA: Sage, 1983.

[32] GREET HOFSTEDE. Culture's Consequences: Comparing Values, Behaviors, Institutions and Organizations Across Nations (Second Edition), Shanghai Foreign Language Education Press, 2008:6

[33] GREET HOFSTEDE. Cultures' Consequences: International Differences in Work Related Values, Sage Publications, Newbury Park, CA, 1980.

[34] GUISETTI M, NICOLADIS E. Gestures and Communicative Development [J]. First Language, 2006, 26:346.

[35] GUDYKUNST W B, & Kim Y Y. Communicating with strangers: an approach to intercultural communication [M]. Mcgraw-Hill Education, 2003.

[36] GUDYKUNST W B, & Kim Y Y. Theories in intercultural communication [M]. Newbury Park: Sage Publications, Inc, 1988.

[37] GUDYKUNST W B, MAYSUMOTO Y, TING-TOOMY S, NISHIDA T, KIM K, HAYMAN S. The influence of cultural individualism-collectivism, self-construal's, and individual values on communication styles across cultures. Human Communication Research, 1996,22:510 - 543.

[38] GUDYKUNST W B, MODY B, KIM Y Y. Methods for Intercultural Communication [M]. Beverly Hills, CA: Sage, 1984.

[39] GUDYKUNST W B, NISHIDA T. The Influence of Cultural Variability on Perception of Communication Behavior Associated With Relationship Terms [J]. Human Communication Research, 1986,13:147 - 166.

[40] GUDYKUNST W B, TING-TOOMY. Verbal Communication Styles [M]. // GUDYKUNST W B, TING-TOOMY (Eds.), Culture and Interpersonal Communication (1988:99 - 115). Newbury Park, CA: Sage.

[41] GUDYKUNST W B(1997). Cultural Variability in Communication: An Introduction [J]. Communication research, 1997,24:327 - 348.

[42] GUDYKUNST W B, MODY B. (Eds.). Handbook of international and intercultural communication [M]. Thousand Oaks, CA: Sage, 2001.

[43] GULLAHORN J T, GULLAHORN J E. (1963). An extension of the U-curve Hypothesis [J]. Journal of Social Issues, 1963,19:33 - 47.

[44] GUO-MING CHEN, William J STAROSTA. Foundations of Intercultural Communication [M]. Shanghai: Shanghai Foreign Language Education Press,

2007:43

[45] HALL E T. The silent language [M]. Garden City, NY: Doubleday, 1959:159-160.

[46] HALL E T. The hidden dimension [M]. Garden City, NY: Doubleday, 1966.

[47] HALL E T. Beyond culture [M]. Garden City, NY: Anchor, 1976.

[48] HALL E T. The dance of life: The other dimension of time [M]. Garden City, NY: Doubleday, 1984.

[49] HALL E T, HALL M R. Understanding Cultural Differences [M]. Yarmouth, ME: Intercultural Press, 1987.

[50] HALL E T. Understanding Cultural Differences: Germans, French and Americans [M]. Yarmouth, ME: Intercultural Press, 1989.

[51] HOFSTEDE G. National cultures in four dimensions [J]. International Studies of Management and Organization, 1983:46-74.

[52] HOFSTEDE G. Culture's Consequences [M]. Beverly Hills, CA: Sage, 1984.

[53] HOVEY J D. Psychological Predictors of Acculturative Stress in Mexican Immigrants [J]. Journal of Psychology, 2000,134:490-502.

[54] HYMES D. Ways of speaking. [M]//R BAUMAN, J SHERZER (Ed.), Explorations in the ethnography of speaking. Cambridge, UK: Cambridge University Press, 1974.

[55] HUMES D. Foundations in Sociolinguistics: An Ethnographic Approach [M]. Philadelphia: University of Pennsylvania Press, 1974.

[56] ISHII S. Thought patterns as modes of rhetoric: The United States and Japan [J]. Communication, 1982,11.

[57] KIM Y Y, GUDYKUNST W B. (Eds.). Cross-cultural adaptation: Current approaches [M]. Beverly Hills: Sage, 1988.

[58] KIM Y Y. Interethnic Conflict: An Interdisciplinary Overview. [J] //J B GITTLER (Ed.). Annual Review of Conflict Knowledge and Conflict Resolution (1989,1). New York: Garland.

[59] KLUCKHOHN C. Mirror of man [M]. New York: McGraw-Hill, 1948.

[60] KLUCKHOHN C, STRODTBECK F. Variations in value orientations [M]. New York: Row, Peterson, 1960.

[61] KLUCKHOHN. The Study of Culture. //D. LERNER, H D LASSWELL (Eds.). The Policy Sciences, 1951/1967:86-101, Stanford, CA: Stanford University Press.

[62] KOHLS L R. Survival kit for overseas living [M]. Yarmouth, ME: Intercultural Press, 1984.

[63] KRAFT C. Worldview in intercultural communication [M]. //F Casmir (Ed.). International and intercultural communication. Washington, DC: University Press of

America, 1978.

[64] KRAMSCH C. Language and culture [M]. London, England: Oxford University Press, 1998.

[65] KROEBER AL, KLUCKHOHN C. Culture: A Critical Review of Concepts and Definitions (1952, vol.47, no.1). Cambridge, MA: Peabody Museum.

[66] LANG J. Creating Architectural Theory: The Role of the Behavioral Sciences in Environmental Design [M]. New York: Van Nostrand Reinhold, 1987.

[67] LANGACKER R. Foundations of Cognitive Grammar, Vol. 1 [M]. Stanford: Stanford University Press, 1987.

[68] LAWRENCE KINCAID. Communication East and West: Points of Departure. [M] // LAWRENCE KINCAID. Communication Theory: Eastern and Western Perspectives. San Diego: Academic Press, 1987.

[69] LEDERER W J, BURDICK E. The Ugly American [M]. Greenwich, CT: Fawcett, 1958.

[70] LI MENYU. The Unique Values of Chinese Traditional Cultural Time Orientation: in comparison with Western Cultural Time Orientation [M]. Intercultural Communication Studies XVII:1, 2008:64 - 70

[71] LUSTIG M W, KOESTER J. Intercultural Competence: Interpersonal communication across cultures [M]. New York: Harper, Collins, 1996.

[72] MCCROSKEY J C. (2006). An Introduction to Rhetorical Communication (9th ed.) [M]. Boston: Allyn & Bacon, 2006.

[73] MANSELL M. Transcultural experience and expressive response [J]. Communication Education, 1981,30:93 - 108.

[74] MARSHALL MCLUHAN. The Gutenberg Galaxy: The Making of Typographic Man [M]. Toronto: University of Toronto Press, 1962.

[75] MATSUMOTO M. The unspoken way: Haragei: Silence in Japanese business and society [M]. New York: Kondansha, 1988.

[76] MEGGERS B J. Environmental limitations on the development of culture. American Anthropologist, 1954,56:801 - 824, IL: Free Press

[77] MIRANDA A O, MATHENY K B. Socio-psychological Predictors and Acculturative Stress Among Latino Adults [J]. Journal of Mental Health Counseling, 2000,22:306 - 318.

[78] NANCY SAKAMOTO, REIKO NAOTSUKA. Polite Fictions: Why Japanese and American Seem to Like Each Other. Tokyo: Kinseido, 1982:80 - 83.

[79] NEULIEP J W. Intercultural communication: A contextual approach [M]. Thousands Oaks, CA: Sage, 1957.

[80] NWAKIORA E, MCADOO H. Acculturative Stress Among Amerasian Refugees: Gender and Racial Differences. Adolescence, 1996,31:477 - 488.

[81] OBERG K. Culture shock and the problems of adjustment to new cultural environments. Practical Anthropology, 1960,7:170 - 179.

[82] OLIVER R T. Communication and culture in ancient India and China. Syracuse, NY: Syracuse University Press, 1971.

[83] PEDERSON D M. Dimensions of Privacy [J]. Perceptual and Motor Skills, 1979,48: 1291 - 1297.

[84] PORTER R E, SAMOVAR L A. An introduction to intercultural communication. // L A SAMOVAR & R E PORTER (Eds.). Intercultural Communication: A reader (1994:4 - 25). Belmont, CA: Wadsworth.

[85] RAPOPORT A. Housing Form and Culture. Eaglewood Cliffs. NJ: Prentice-Hall, 1969.

[86] RICHARD W FISHER. Globalization's Impact on U. S. Growth and Inflation. Remarks before the Dellas, TX State Assembly, May 22, 2006. Accessed December 17, 2007, from http://www. dallasfed. Org/news/speeches/fisher/2006/fs060522. cfm.

[87] ROGERS E M, STEINFATT T M. Intercultural Communication. Waveland press, Inc. , Illinois, 1999.

[88] SAMOVAR L A, PORTER R E. Communication between cultures. Belmont, CA: Wadsworth, 1995.

[89] SAMOVAR L A, PORTER R E. Intercultural communication: a reader. Belmont, CA: Wadsworth, 2000.

[90] SAPIR E. (Ed.). Language: An introduction to the study of speech. New York: Harcourt, Brace & World, 1921.

[91] SCHLESINGER A M. The Disuniting of America: Reflections of a Multicultural Society. New York: Norton, 1993:10.

[92] SCHWARTZ S. (1990). Individualism-collectivism [J]. Journal of Cross-Cultural Psychology, 1990,21:139 - 151.

[93] SHOTTER J. Wittgenstein and Psychology: on our "hook-up" to reality. //A Phillips-Griffiths (Eds.). The Wittgenstein Centenary Lectures, Cambridge: Cambridge University Press, 1991:193 - 208

[94] SITARAM K S, HAAPANEN L W. 1979, The Role of Values in Intercultural Communication. //M K ASANTE & C A Blake (Eds). The Handbook of Intercultural Communication, 1979:147 - 160, Beverly Hills, CA: Sage.

[95] SPITZBERG B H. A Model of Intercultural Competence. [M] // L A SAMOVAR,

R E PORTER (Eds.). Intercultural Communication Reader (8th ed). Belmont, CA: Wadsworth, 1977:379 - 391.

[96] SPITZBERG B H, CUPACH W R. Interpersonal Communication Competence [M]. Beverly Hills, CA: Sage, 1984.

[97] SPITZBERG B H. Communication Competence: Measures of Perceived Effectiveness. //A Handbook for the Study of Human Communication, ed. Charles H. Tardy. Norwood, NJ: Albex, 1988:67 - 105.

[98] STORTI C. Cross-Cultural Dialogues: 74 Brief Encounters with Cultural Differences. Yarmouth, ME: Intercultural Press, 1994.

[99] THOMAS K W, KILMANN R H. Thomas-Kilmann Conflict Mode Instrument. New York: XICOM, 1974.

[100] TING-TOOMY S. A face negotiation theory. //Y. Kim, W GUDYKUNST (Eds.). Theories in intercultural communication. Newbury Park, CA: Sage, 1988.

[101] TING-TOOMEY S. Communicating across cultures [M]. New York, NY: Guilford Press, 1999.

[102] TING-TOOMEY S. Managing intercultural conflicts effectively. //L A SAMOVAR, R E PORTER (Eds.). Intercultural communication: A Reader. Belmont, CA: Wadsworth, 1994.

[103] TING-TOOMEY S. Toward a theory of conflict and culture. //W GUDYKUNST, L STEWART, S Ting-Toomey (Eds.). Communication, culture, and organizational processes. Beverly Hills, CA: Sage, 1985:71 - 86.

[104] TRIANDIS H C. The Self and Social Behavior in Differing Cultural Contexts [J]. Psychological Review, 1989,96:506 - 520.

[105] TURNER C V. The Sinasina "Big Man" complex: A central culture theme [J]. Practical Anthropology, 1968,15:16 - 23.

[106] VARNER I, L BEAMER. Intercultural Communication in the Global Workplace, 3rd ED., NY: McGraw-Hill, 2005.

[107] WHORF B. (1940). Linguistics as an Exact Science [J]. Technology Review, 1940, 45:61 - 63

[108] YOUNG L. Crosstalk and culture in Sino-American communication [M]. Cambridge, UK: Cambridge University Press, 1994.

[109] YUM J O. (1997). The Impact of Confucianism on Interpersonal Relationships and Communication Patterns in East Asia. //L A SAMOVAR, R E PORTER (Eds.). Intercultural Communication: A Reader. Belmont, CA: Wadsworth, 1997:78 - 88.

[110] 常俊跃，霍跃红，姚璐，赵永青. 中国文化(英文版)[M]. 北京：北京大学出版社，2011.

[111] 陈国明. 跨文化传播的脉络性. 跨文化交际研究(第三辑)[J]. 北京：高等教育出版

社，2012.
[112] 戴炜栋.新编简明英语语言学教程[M].上海：上海外语教育出版社，2002.
[113] 戴晓东.跨文化交际理论[M].上海：上海外语教育出版社，2011.
[114] 邓辉.世界文化地理[M].北京：北京大学出版社，2010.
[115] 胡嘉渝，彭旭，阮宇翔，董贺轩.城市与建筑专业英语[M].天津：天津大学出版社，2010.
[116] 胡兆亮，阿尔斯郎，琼达.中国文化地理概述[M].北京：北京大学出版社，2009.
[117] 贾玉新.跨文化交际学[M].上海：上海外语教育出版社，1997.
[118] 姜望琪.语用学——理论及应用[M].北京：北京大学出版社，2000.
[119] 金磊，李沉.中外建筑与文化[M].北京：科学技术文献出版社，2006.
[120] 李建军，李贵苍.跨文化交际[M].武汉：武汉大学出版社，2011.
[121] 李建中.中国文化概论[M].武汉：武汉大学出版社，2005.
[122] 王玉环，李金珊.跨文化交际学教程[M].北京：北京大学出版社，2011.
[123] 杨敏，王克奇，王恒展.中国文化通览[M].北京：高等教育出版社，2006.

Keys to Exercises

Chapter One

II. Multiple Choice

1. A 2. D 3. B 4. D 5. C

III. Fill in the blanks with the words given in the bank.

1. B 2. D 3. C 4. A 5. B 6. C 7. A 8. B 9. D 10. A

Chapter Two

II. Multiple Choice

1. A 2. C 3. B 4. C 5. D

III. Fill in the blanks with the words given in the bank.

1. context 2. usage 3. cultivation 4. agriculture 5. refer 6. education
7. anthropology 8. society 9. material 10. referent

Chapter Three

II. Multiple Choice

1. A 2. D 3. C 4. C 5. B

III. Comprehension Check

1. T 2. F 3. T 4. F 5. T 6. F 7. T 8. F

Chapter Four

II. Multiple Choice

1. C 2. D 3. D 4. B 5. A

III. Comprehension Check

1. F 2. T 3. T 4. F 5. T 6. T 7. F 8. F

Chapter Five

II. Comprehension Check

1. T 2. F 3. F 4. T 5. T 6. F 7. T 8. T

III. Fill in the blanks with the words given in the bank.

1. source 2. decoding 3. respond 4. interpretive 5. information 6. apprehension 7. styles 8. explicit 9. indirect 10. community

Unit Six

II. Comprehension Check

1. T 2. T 3. F 4. T 5. T 6. F 7. F 8. T

III. Fill in the blanks with the words given in the bank.

1. imitate; 2. symbolic; 3. creative; 4. rule-governed; 5. dynamic; 6. complicated; 7. context; 8. intertwined; 9. mould; 10. reality

Chapter Seven

II. Multiple Choice

1. A 2. D 3. B 4. C 5. B

III. Comprehension Check

1. F 2. F 3. F 4. T 5. T 6. F 7. F 8. T

Chapter Eight

II. Multiple Choice

1. C 2. B 3. D 4. C 5. D

III. Comprehension Check

1. T 2. F 3. F 4. F 5. F 6. T 7. T 8. F